## Cataloging-in-Publication Data

378.1     O'Brien, Patrick Sean, 1963 Jan. 21-
OBR       Making college count : a real world look at how to succeed in
          and after college / Patrick S. O'Brien. - Cincinnati, Ohio :
          Student Success Inc., © 1999.

          157 p. : ill. ; 20.9 cm.

          Summary: A handbook for college students, designed to teach
          them how to succeed in college and best prepare themselves to
          get the job they want upon graduation.

          ISBN 0-9633678-3-8 (pbk.)

          1. College student orientation - United States   2. College stu-
          dents - United States - Psychology   3. Success   I. Title

                                                        96-094706
          LB2343.32

                                                        378.1'98_dc21

*More advance*

# PRAISE FOR
## *Making College Count*

"Making College Count draws an 'on-the-money' connection between college and career...and gives practical, no-nonsense advice on how to make the connection work."

- James M. Holec, Jr.
**Management Consulting Partner, PricewaterhouseCoopers**

"Making College Count deserves a place on the shelves of every high school library and should be required reading for every graduating senior. Blessedly more of a conversation than a lecture, it is part reality-check and part self-help manual for those looking to make the most of their college years."

- Dianne Young
**Senior Writer, Southern Living**

"An easy guide that can, in an hour or two, help students avoid wasting years of their life or wasting opportunities of a lifetime."

- Randy Scott
**Vice President Marketing, Nine West Group, Inc.**

"A book like this is long overdue. I'm sorry it did not exist when I went to college. It's TERRIFIC."

- Michael Grossman
**President, Rim Pacific Imports**

"It is indeed encouraging to read something that can be of GREAT assistance to our youth who are willing to make the commitment. <u>Making College Count</u> is an excellent piece of work and should be must reading for all who are considering a college education."

- J.B. "Jack" Curcio
**Retired-President, Chairman, Mack Trucks, Inc.**

"As president of a successful, entrepreneurial company as well as a father with two children in college, I feel this book is a <u>must read</u> for college freshmen. All the principles that helped jump start my career are here and they're presented in a way that appeals to students. Both my son and daughter enjoyed the book and felt it was a tremendous asset."

- Roger Kimps
**President & C.E.O., Graphic Management Corporation**

"The book offers no easy road to success; however, it will help future college students avoid the pitfalls many students stumble into. Pat has explained in a very readable form practices and approaches that worked well for him, and should work well for all students entering college today."

- Dr. David Sink
**President, Blue Ridge Community College**

"Having interviewed and recruited hundreds of individuals during my career, I feel confident saying the principles of this book are right on target. I would strongly recommend it for students serious about success in college and, more importantly, after graduation."

- Larry Baker
**Sr. Vice President Administration, Wausau Papers**

"Very insightful. Timeless wisdom combined with some very innovative thoughts. All in a very student-friendly format."

- Carlos Rodriquez
**Vice President Operations, Vincam**
**Harvard Business School Graduate**

"I particularly liked the way it linked school to the job market and the concept of making your time count. It is a good life lesson...work hard and have fun too! The Winning Characteristics are right on the mark and are what employers are looking for."

-Lori Glander
**Training & Development Specialist, MILSCO Manufacturing Corporation**

"All the things you want your children to know and understand, but must hear it from another person. I have made it a 'must read' for our six children. It provides extremely valuable information that can be as important as the diploma itself."

-Tom Fazio
**World's Leading Golf Course Architect**

"No matter which career path you plan to pursue, this book will help get you to wherever you want to go."

-Tom Southworth
**Counselor, Wausau East High School**

"Making College Count should be required reading for every high school student! Reading the book is like having a one on one conversation with a mentor that really knows what lies ahead for a student, and also knows how a student can get a "jump-start" in his/her life."

-Duane McKibbin
**President/Owner Henderson Oil Co., Inc.**
**Stanford University Graduate School of Business, MBA**

"Must reading for every teenager, college student and young career-starter, it answers the common question, 'What am I doing and why?' "

-Bill Lattimore
**President - The Branigar Organization, Inc.**

"I have been recruiting senior level management for corporations since 1983. During this time I have found that out of the thousands of people I have interviewed, approximately 90% of them did not have any idea as to what they should pursue in college. Similarly, the same percentage today are employed in a different profession than the major they pursued in college. This book gives clear focus on positioning yourself to a rewarding career after college. It takes the guesswork out of your career direction. Well done! This book should be a required course in high school."

-Dennis J. Caruso
Managing Partner - Caruso & Associates, Inc. - Executive Search Consultants.

"The tools in this book are right on. These principles are what set me apart from my peers. Every college student should read this book."

-Carmen Nagy
New Hire - Andersen Consulting

"With the significant financial commitment involved in attending college today, a book such as Making College Count offers its readers a game plan that will ultimately protect their college investment."

-Laura Hardy
Southern Regional Campaign Director
Juvenile Diabetes Foundation International

"Making College Count is the "In Search of Excellence" of college preparation books. Well-organized and written in an incredibly easy to read style, this book is sure to be must reading for anyone contemplating a college education."

-Chuck Mitchell
Senior Vice President - The Branigar Organization, Inc.

"Given my extensive involvement in education, I'm very excited about Making College Count and the positive impact it will have on today's students."

-Julie Pyburn
Educational Speaker and Consultant

"The author's insights and advice amount to the keys to success in today's competitive job market. My former students who have been the top targets of recruiters have achieved that lofty status by preparing themselves in the manner so eloquently described by the author. Making College Count is required reading for my own teenagers as they are starting to make their college and career choices."

-Donald G. Norris Ph.D.
**Associate Marketing Professor - Miami University**
**University of California, Berkeley**


"Having spent two years with Pat as his college roommate and close friend, I can say that his philosophies and principles are practical and sound! Simply put, his plan works!"

-Joe Williams
**Sales Manager - Schlage Lock Company**


"As someone who interviews students as part of the college admission process, I know this book will provide much-needed guidance - a must for anyone who wants to know how to major in 'life'."

-John L. Jacobus
**General Counsel, JPC, Inc. - Harvard Law School Graduate**


"Having been involved in the start-up of four automobile plants, I have interviewed more than 500 college graduates. How great it would have been if all those candidates had used this book as a guide earlier in their careers."

-Allen Kinzer
**President, BMW Manufacturing**


"It provides realistic tools in a step-by-step sequence that is very user-friendly. This is a valuable resource for students and those who work with students."

-Paulie McCown
**Director of Guidance Counselors, Whitefish Bay High School**

# Making
# COLLEGE COUNT ™

First Print..............December 1996
Second Print..............April 1997
Third Print..............April 1998
Fourth Print..............July 1999
Fifth Print..............April 2000
Sixth Print..............July 2001

Published by

**monster.com**
5 Clock Tower Place
Suite 300
Maynard, MA 01754

Illustrations by: Pete Adams
Design by: Patricia Dvorak

Printed in the United States of America
Library of Congress Catalog Card Number: 96-094706
ISBN 0-9633678-3-8

*www.makingcollegecount.com*

# *Table of* CONTENTS

# *Necessary* THANKS

*T*hanks to the literally thousands of business and professional leaders, college officials, high school guidance counselors, job interviewees, parents, students, and friends whose thoughts and ideas have helped shape this book.

Thanks also to the 200 or so people who survived the interview process and have actually had to work for me over the last 10 years. Each of them has added to the thoughts and ideas in <u>Making College Count</u>.

Special thanks go to three close friends, Brad Baker, Marilyn Muldowney (now my wife), and Barb Miller. With tremendously successful careers after earning degrees from Harvard, Ithaca College, and Vanderbilt respectively, they have added greatly to the book.

I also want to thank in advance the many people who will call or write to offer their assistance as a "much needed" editor for this book. Let me respond up front by saying that the book is meant to "talk" to you. To accomplish this required taking a few liberties with the rules of grammar. I do know "proper" English. I just didn't want it to get in the way of our "conversation."

# So who is THIS GUY?

**W**here do I start?

Writing about how to use college to build your successful future is much easier than writing about myself. But I do think it's necessary to give you an understanding of who I am and what I'm about to lend a bit of credibility to the chapters that follow. So here goes.

My name is Pat O'Brien.

Prior to going to college, I was pretty much focused on having fun and getting through high school with a minimal amount of effort. Skimming my notes in study hall and homeroom was my idea of "hitting the books" for a test. Playing football, frying fish at Long John Silvers, and driving my 12 year old Mustang were the extent of my extracurricular activities.

My grades in high school were decent, a bit above a 3.0. Given that, I thought I was doing just fine, doing what was necessary to stay ahead of the pack. I was accepted at Miami University (in Ohio) and was ready to go get an education and have some serious fun living on my own.

Leading up to my graduation, I was mentally gearing up for a summer of working 60 to 70 hours a week pulling weeds for Sandy's Landscaping to help pay for my education. My folks would also contribute and I would take on some major student loan debt to pay the remainder. I was more than willing to do this, though, because I "knew" that I'd get a great job after I got my degree.

Then came my wake up call — my high school senior class awards assembly. It was the type of event that you would typically sleep through, but I left it feeling like I'd been hit in the stomach with a baseball bat.

Fellow classmates were honored for scholarships they had received. I was blown away at the tens of thousands of dollars in awards being announced. "Full-ride" and partial scholarships were acknowledged, not just for athletics but for "outstanding academic achievement," a fancy way of saying good grades.

What did I get? Nothing — nothing but a horrible realization that I'd be pulling weeds and going into big debt to do the same thing they'd be doing for free or at a reduced cost. It was a crystal clear message that I was not leading the pack, I was well back in it.

Two thoughts raced through my head. The first was that this whole situation was terribly unfair! These people weren't brilliant. I should have been getting at least a <u>little</u> of all this "free money."

The second thought was that these same people, and people like them, would be getting the jobs that I wanted four years from then if I didn't somehow turn the tables. I decided that day to do whatever it took in college to be first in line for a great job when I graduated.

It was a big day in my life.

It would still be a couple of years before I had a solid understanding of what the real keys were to being first in line. In the interim, I made some educated guesses and substituted hard work for knowledge,

when necessary. As I did this, I constantly searched for the answers – watching successful students and talking to countless professors and professionals, learning what I needed to know to make college count.

After an extremely enjoyable four years of school, I started my career at Procter and Gamble in its brand management/marketing area. It was a highly sought-after position and one that offered one of the best opportunities (and starting salaries) possible out of school.

About 60% of the people hired for that job that year had MBA's from big name schools. Another 25% or so came from Ivy League schools. The competition was intense, to say the least.

Adding to the uniqueness of the situation, it wasn't even a job I actively pursued. They came after me based on my resumé. Based on my strong record, I was (at least on paper) the type of candidate they wanted.

Another point worth mentioning is that I interviewed for five jobs and received four offers, all from strong companies. Said another way, the principles in this book can open doors – the doors that <u>you</u> want to open.

Three years after graduation, I was a Procter and Gamble Brand Manager, helping to run the $400,000,000 Crest toothpaste business. At age 25, I was one of the youngest managers in company history to hold that job.

I worked hard to achieve this, but I never would have had the opportunity to do so if I didn't have the record in college that got me the interview.

Another important aspect of my career development was that in the Brand Manager role, I had the opportunity to begin sitting on the other side of the interview desk. After extensive training, I was out talking to college seniors who wanted to come to work for Procter and Gamble.

After I had interviewed over 50 candidates in that first year alone, my thoughts on what made up the perfect candidate crystallized in my head. Only then did I realize how good my choices had been, and how critical smart choices in college are for success in the job search process.

At age 27, I left Procter and Gamble to become the Director of Marketing for The Branigar Organization, a developer of private country club communities in the southeastern U.S. I lived in and nationally marketed an island community off the coast of Savannah.

At age 30, I was promoted to Vice President and Project Director at Champion Hills, a new community in the mountains of western North Carolina. This role included managing a $20,000,000 real estate development operation, a country club, a property owners' association, and a staff of 90 employees. I interviewed, hired, and managed people in a wide range of occupations. But regardless of whether it was an executive chef, security chief, construction manager, horticulturalist, or financial controller, I always looked to see if the candidates exhibited a set of "Winning Characteristics" before I hired them. (More on that later).

While I was there, the idea of Making College Count went from being an idea that I might pursue "someday" to something of great interest to me. I discussed it with parents and students, as well as leaders in business, law, education, and other fields, and received strong encouragement to fully develop the program. So, at age 33, I retired from corporate America to develop Making College Count into a complete learning program, including seminars, books, tapes, workbooks, and planning calendars to benefit today's student. And, thus far, I am thoroughly enjoying it.

For me, this career path has been rewarding and consistent with where I have wanted to go. You may define success very differently. That's okay. What's key is creating the opportunity to achieve <u>your</u> success.

What has worked for me? A lot of work, some good decision making, and a little luck. One thing I'm certain of, though, is that it was the principles in this book that put me in that great first job and gave me the chance to show what I could do.

*While there are no guarantees in life (or this book), with your commitment, the* **IDEAS** *that follow* **SHOULD HELP GIVE YOU THAT SAME OPPORTUNITY.**

# *The Rules of the game*

*B*efore you do anything, if you plan to do it well, you learn what defines success, how difficult it is to achieve it, and what the rules are. It only makes sense. Your college experience should be no different.

The following three chapters will confirm that you and I are in sync on what the objectives of college are and will let you know how the ultimate judges, your potential future employers, view the process.

Unfortunately, it will also give you a few statistics on how well today's students are making out. I'll give you a hint. They're not pretty.

Understanding all this now, as opposed to after your senior year, will help you make smarter decisions during your days at college. It's really very simple and quite logical. If you understand what the judges define as success, what your odds are of achieving it, and how the rules have been set, you're more likely to make it happen than if you don't.

> *There is no ONE right way to be "successful" in (or after) college.*

*They're crashin' and burnin' out there.*

One more point. There's no <u>one</u> right way to be "successful" in (or after) college. There can't be, because everyone defines success differently.

You'll be introduced to a broad range of concepts in this book. <u>All</u> of them won't be right for you. But they are <u>proven</u> approaches. They do work. As such, they'll give you a strong framework. Your personal interests and strengths will guide you in how to make them work for you (and in when you'll want to take a different approach).

By the way, if you haven't read the "So Who is This Guy?" section, please take a quick look through it. Hopefully it will communicate a few things to you.

## I've been there. I've done it. I can help you.
# SO LISTEN UP.

# Chapter 1

# Why are you GOING TO COLLEGE?

*A* good question and a good place to start. If single-handedly saving the world or getting an education <u>solely</u> for education's sake is what you're all about, let me save you some time. Don't read this book; it's not for you.

On the other hand, if you'd like your college experience to be a building process – elevating you to the most interesting, challenging, financially rewarding job you can get in your chosen field – then you're in the right place.

Don't get me wrong. I think learning simply for the sake of learning is a worthwhile objective. Really, it is. In fact, I'll probably go back to school at some point for just that reason. You can never know too much and you should always be in a learning mode in life.

The key difference here is that I'll take that step <u>after</u> I have accomplished my professional goals and achieved my financial objectives. I will not undertake this endeavor as a means of getting there.

*If you're shooting for the stars, read on.*

Let's look at a "real life" scenario that brings the issue to life. During my senior year I had a choice between going to a class lecture or a pre-interview reception thrown by Procter and Gamble. The decision, for me, was easy. I went to the reception. It's simply a matter of priorities. I ask again...why are you going to college?

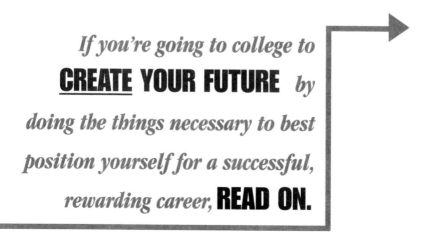

*If you're going to college to* **CREATE YOUR FUTURE** *by doing the things necessary to best position yourself for a successful, rewarding career,* **READ ON.**

# Chapter 2

# The Cold

# HARD FACTS

$S$trap on your seat belt. You're in for a rough chapter.

While building your future is your goal, it is important that you know that the landscape is littered with students who are still looking for a building site.

Adding to that, the cost of the construction is itself skyrocketing. And finally, the difference in earnings between those who did and did not have a successful effort is large and growing.

Did I mention that it's tough out there?

Let's first look at the success statistics. As I mentioned, they're kind of ugly. Based on numbers released in 1998 by American College Testing (ACT):

- Only 73% of freshmen will return as sophomores.

- Among private schools, the number is only 74% (not much better).

- Only 26% will graduate in 4 years (a bit depressing).
- Another 28% will graduate in 5 years (we're still only at about half).

Now let's lay a U.S. Bureau of Labor Statistics projection on top of that.

- Only two in three of those that do graduate will get a job that required a degree.

Do the math. Only 36% of incoming freshmen will graduate in 5 years or less and get a job that required a degree.

Not pretty.

*The magnitude of the challenge can be overwhelming.*

And, the cost of failure is higher than ever. The average total cost (tuition, room and board, books, fees, etc.) for a student in 1998 was approaching $10,000 for a state school and close to $30,000 for a private one (College Board). These costs have risen about 10% a year on average over the past 10 years. Multiply that by four or five years and that's a lot of money to spend to get a job flipping burgers.

Again, tough numbers.

Further complicating the issue, a college degree is now more important than ever from an earnings standpoint. Based on U.S. Labor Department statistics, a typical college graduate established in the work force now makes almost <u>double</u> what a non-graduate makes. And, the spread between the two is growing dramatically.

<u>Average Annual Income</u>
(U.S. Adults age 25+)

| College Graduate | $50,100 |
| High School Graduate | $26,200 |

And last but not least:

•25% of 25 year olds are now still living with their parents (oh what fun!).

There are two ways to look at these statistics. The first is that the situation is hopeless. It's not. The other is that there is a WHOLE LOT to be said for doing what is necessary in college to graduate and build <u>your</u> successful future.

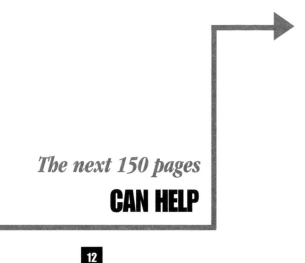

*The next 150 pages*
**CAN HELP**

# Chapter 3

# Building

# YOUR FUTURE

*T*wo hours from now you're going to look at college in a whole new way. You're going to look at it through the eyes of an interviewer, seeing opportunities (and pitfalls) that you didn't even know existed.

You'll think differently about what's important to do there, and have insights that some other less successful students may not have for many years after they move on to flipping burgers at Burgerama. You'll know it's a little more than showing up and trying to get good grades.

You'll think of college as an opportunity to build a successful future.

Along with getting a piece of paper to frame on your wall (that's a diploma), the objective of college, in my humble opinion, is to build a track record loaded with the things that employers (or grad schools) are looking for. In this book, we'll call them the "Winning Characteristics" and explain them to you in significant detail. Nothing you will do in college will be more important than developing these traits and being able to demonstrate that you possess them.

You'll have three ways to do this — with your performance inside the classroom, via extracurricular activities outside the classroom, and through meaningful work experience. Each of them is a tremendous opportunity to develop, sharpen, and exhibit these Winning Characteristics.

Now, to accomplish this, you'll need to take care of some basics. Along with picking a school and a major, you'll need to master a few critical skills that will allow you to take on the complex challenges that will face you during your college experience. This book will help you do that.

Then, with those basics in your grasp, your academics, extracurriculars, and employment experiences will be your golden opportunities to develop and impressively exhibit the Winning Characteristics. Each will be a part of the foundation upon which you'll build your successful future.

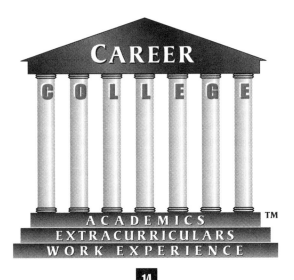

*It is a* **PROVEN, SOLID STRUCTURE FOR SUCCESS,** *one that will allow you go wherever you want to go.*

# If you're not there yet.

*I* f you're already in college or have picked your school and major with a high degree of certainty, you can just skim the next two chapters. You've already been through the thought process (I hope) that will be shared in these sections. If not, read on.

What do you want to do for the majority of your waking hours for the next 40 or so years? What field will leverage your unique personality and skills and allow you to jump out of bed each day and feel good about what you'll be doing that day? More simply put, just what is it that's going to make you happy?

Following from that, what school is going to put you in the best position to interview for (and get) a great entry level position in that field – or in a field that you decide two years from now is a much better place for you to be?

*What do you want to do for the next 40 or so years?*

The issues are among the most complex you've ever faced. And, the information you need to help you make the decision may not seem readily available.

*A given interest can take you many different places.*

With an investment of your time, there is a <u>tremendous</u> amount of information available to assist you in the process.

And remember, nobody is going to give you the answers. To determine what is best to you, <u>you</u> need to take an active interest and lead the process.

**Remember, it's your life.**

# AND YOUR CAREER.

# Choosing

# Chapter 4

# YOUR MAJOR

*I* could write a whole book on this subject. In fact, others already have. If you're interested in one to help you understand what type of career might be best for you, <u>What Color is My Parachute?</u> can help. It's a book that's been around forever, but the message still rings true. Or, high school and college counselors have some pretty good tests to help you understand what field might be the best fit for your interests and talents.

Let me share several thoughts about this critical area and see if I can help simplify the process for you. First, pick something you fundamentally enjoy. It doesn't matter if you hear about a sales job where you could eventually earn up to a quarter of a million dollars a year. If you're not comfortable with people you don't know, are not outgoing by nature, and hate the idea of travel, odds are you won't be successful or happy in that role. Second, pick something you think that you would be particularly good at. It will be difficult for you to be the next Sheryl Crow if you can't carry a tune.

I would also definitely recommend that you talk to

professors or professionals in a field you're considering to understand the quality and quantity of jobs available that relate to that major. For instance, if you like mythology, it's much better to find out sooner than later that, unless you want to teach mythology, there are not an overabundance of good  jobs available that directly utilize this degree.

Sometimes the best decision is no decision at all (at least for a little while). Some schools will allow you to be an "undeclared" major. If you have no idea what you want to do, this can be a legitimate way to delay a decision. It may allow you to take a wide range of classes your freshman year and get a taste of a variety of subjects (and do a full year of research) before making this call.

There are two things to strongly consider before taking this path. First, will you still be able to graduate "on time" (typically in four years)? And second, will the school penalize you in any way (like not letting you into some high demand majors) because you delayed making your choice? A counselor at the college can give you good insight here.

Let's take the undeclared major concept to an extreme. An acquaintance of mine has been in college for six years and does not currently have a major. He's had a couple already but doesn't seem to be comfortable making a career choice. This is not a good thing. It's expensive and can eat up your life.

After freshman year, <u>make a call</u>. If later on you think you made a mistake, change majors <u>once</u>. Get a degree. Get some real world experience. Then if you want to make a move, you'll have a solid experience base to build upon.

While there is no such thing as a "bad" major, you need to understand that a specific employer will often only consider students from related majors to fill a job. This happens most often with jobs with a technical element, ranging from computer science and engineering to accounting and health care.

The concern with some fields of study is their day- to-day applicability to the "highest demand" fields in the "real world." Some like English, economics, and math have strong "across the board" appeal. But if after graduation you want to go to work for a small organization or even start your own company, studying French literature or psychology might not get you as far as some other choices of major.

Here's the distinction. Large firms and graduate schools plan to teach you the specific skills you'll need for future employment. When I interviewed for my job at Procter and Gamble, the recruiters told me that they didn't care about my lack of marketing course work. They felt the company knew more about marketing than many colleges and would teach me what I needed to know <u>after</u> I got the job. Obviously, in this case, almost any major would have been just fine.

Now let's look at the other side of the coin. Most of the job growth in the future is projected to come from small companies. In fact, since 1990, small companies have created 10 million jobs. Big company employment has actually declined. Given that, you're more likely to go to work for a small company than graduates of the past.

Small organizations can not afford the comprehensive training programs that big companies offer. They will therefore be more interested in hiring someone who has an education that is more specifically related to and more relevant to the particular position they are trying to fill.

One final point in this area. Many majors will qualify you for a broad range of jobs, However, studying in a very "general" major should not be used as a vehicle to allow you to <u>not</u> make a decision as to what you want to do after college. Any choice of majors will open some doors but will close others. Whether you realize it or not, you <u>will</u> be making some decisions about your future by picking <u>any</u> major. So make them wisely.

Getting back to the general subject, picking a major can be difficult and nerve-racking. How can you decide what you want to do before you ever do it? What if you make the wrong choice?

After you do pick a major and have moved into the stage of second guessing yourself (almost everyone does), here are three things to think about.

First, everyone else is just as confused as you are. They're just not talking about it.

Second, if you can possibly get one, an internship will shed some light on the issue. It will give you a much better understanding of the type of work you would actually be doing in a particular field. I'll talk more about internships later in the book.

Third, do not feel limited by your major. You can interview for and get a job outside of your major with larger companies if you follow the principles in <u>Making College Count</u>. I did.

In my case, I had a double major of finance and accounting. After an accounting internship at a bank, I had serious doubts as to whether accounting was what I wanted to do with the rest of my life. It was a great job in a high-potential field. It was a great company. It just wasn't what I wanted to do every day for the next 40 years.

I did not change my major as I was committed to graduating in four years (mostly because I had very little money). I instead interviewed not only for finance and accounting jobs, but for marketing, consulting, and sales positions as well. As you know (if you read the "So Who is This Guy" section), I was offered and took a job in marketing.

Another point worth making is that you are not bound for life to your major even if you take your first job in that field. Many people move from

one department to another in an organization after they find that their previously chosen field is not right for them. In fact, having a couple of different departmental perspectives can be a real advantage to an employee working in a team setting.

And, with technology changing as fast as it is, the odds are you won't take only one job and retire from it when you turn 65 anyway. Even if you are one of the unlikely few who will stay with one company for the next 40 years, you will play a variety of roles for them during that extended time frame.

*So, choosing a major is important.*

*But contrary to popular belief,*

*you're* **NOT MAKING A DECISION**

*that* **YOU'LL HAVE TO LIVE WITH**

*for the rest of your life.*

# Chapter 5

# YOUR SCHOOL

*S*tart with the finish line in your sight.

You want to get a great job coming out of college. Pick the school best positioned to help you do this. The social element of college is also important and shouldn't be overlooked. But, picking a school just because it's in a fun city, has a top ten football team, or has a reputation for great parties is probably not a brilliant move. Bottom line, you'll make great friends and have a lot of fun at any school you pick, so let's focus on the meatier issues.

If you have some feel as to what area of study you want to go into (natural science, architecture, business, health care, etc.), find out what schools have a good reputation in that field. A counselor can be a big help in doing this. On the subject of counselors, if you're already utilizing them, keep doing so. If you aren't, you'll need to get over your fear of "adults" trying to offer "guidance." They have a great deal of meaningful information and perspective to share.

Along with counselors, talk to anyone you know who is in that field or even currently in college studying to enter it. They will have some good real world insight on the subject.

And, even if you can afford a private school, don't overlook public school opportunities. A public school may be outstanding in your particular field of interest.

One key thing to mention here is that if you are uncertain about your major, you'll want to choose a school that is not too specialized, one that will give you many different options if you decide to change your major. Going to a specialized nursing school is not a big idea if you're not sure you want to be a nurse.

If you really don't know what you want to do, find out if a school you are considering will take applications with "undeclared" majors. Some will throw them away, never considering a potentially strong candidate only because he or she "lacks direction." On a related note, find out how difficult it is at a given school to <u>change</u> your major. Some schools make it easy. Others make it extremely difficult.

At the end of your junior year in high school, you should begin writing to the admissions offices of schools you are considering to get information and an application. Many schools will send you information on their own, possibly adding to the list of options you actively pursue. One other convenient place you can find information is on the internet. Most schools now have more information on their web sites than they do in their brochures.

After you dig through the initial information, you'll need to narrow your options. Discard schools that are unappealing to you. Try to find friends or older brothers and sisters of friends who are attending candidate schools to get their perspective. Go to the library or get on the internet to see what has been written on the schools in recent magazines and newspapers.

SCHOOL INFO

Utilize the guides to colleges available at your local bookstore. They are thorough, well organized, and can save you a tremendous amount of leg work. Yes, this process requires a little work, but you'll be amazed by how much you'll learn.

If you are still confused, in need of some extra guidance, or attempting to get into an exclusive school, college admissions counselors can be a good resource. Their services will not be free, but good counselors can be a big help.

Visit the schools you are considering. Talk to some of the students who are enrolled there. Sit in on a class or two to get a feel for the place. And, back to our objective of setting yourself up for a great job, spend some time at their Career Planning and Placement Office. Find out who interviews there and get any data the office may have on the success their past graduates have had in getting jobs before and after graduation. Find out why they think their students do well in landing great jobs. Don't be shy. This is a big decision.

Let me mention the importance of timing. At many schools you will enhance your odds of acceptance with early application. There is a certain logic to this because when the school is down to its last few slots, it can afford to be extremely selective.

Also, it is a good idea to apply to several schools, or two at a minimum. I would suggest both a "stretch" and a "safety" school. The stretch school should be one of the top schools in your field of interest. Even if you don't think you can afford it, give it a try. If you're a strong candidate, the school may be able to provide more financial aid than you had anticipated.

The safety school should be one that you have a high degree of confidence will admit you. The safety school application will help ensure that you won't be sitting at home when your friends go off to school in the fall.

A couple of other points worth covering...

First, if you think you'll want or need a lot of personal attention, you'll want to strongly consider a small school or a small program within a big school. If you want to be able to ask questions freely or spend quality time one-on-one with your professor, this will be more easily accomplished at a small school or in a small program at a big school.

On the other hand, if you don't think you will require a lot of personal time or attention, a big program or a large school can be an excellent option. Sometimes it will have recognized leaders in a field as professors while a small school may not. Said another way, a world renowned scientist may be more likely to teach at a large or prestigious school than at a small regional college.

Second, take the application process seriously. Spend a good amount of time on your application to make sure that you're presenting yourself as well as you can. The upcoming section on the "Winning Characteristics" will give you a feel for the types of things a college may be looking for in a candidate. If you're in doubt, admissions counselors can be helpful here, as well.

Unless the school conducts interviews (some prestigious ones do), your application will be your only opportunity to show your stuff. Have several people read it, checking for proper grammar and spelling. You don't want to appear to be careless or not genuinely interested. It does make a difference.

Third, if you think you'll want to study abroad for a semester or a year, research the subject as a part of your decision making process. Interest in this has increased as we have moved toward a "global economy," and some schools are better set up than others to offer opportunities in this area.

Fourth, plan on feeling as if you made a big mistake after you've been at college for a month. Wait at least a semester to decide if you've chosen the right school. Most freshmen who are living away from home for the first time begin to miss their family, their old friends, and even the family mutt after a few weeks of their newfound freedom.

And, dining hall food and laundry get old in a hurry. It will take you a full semester, if not a full year, to settle in and know whether or not you chose the right school.

*And, take at least some comfort in the fact that* **WHAT YOU ACCOMPLISH** *while you're in college is probably more* **IMPORTANT** *than the school at which you accomplish it.*

# The winning characteristics

*"T*his is the job. The right organization. The right people. The right work. And, the right salary."

"Now, how am I going to get it?"

This is a thought pondered for the first time all too often by second semester college seniors who are attempting to sharpen their interviewing skills.

"What is the magic answer that will separate me from the other 15 students they'll talk to on that day?" Is it the best response to that dreaded question "What would your friends say is your biggest weakness?"

Is it the proper shine on your shoes? Is it a conservative maroon tie or bow on a well starched white shirt or blouse? Or is it whether your resumé is typed in the right font style or printed on white or tan paper?

*It will take years to develop them, not a few weeks or months.*

Unfortunately, for all but a few of the individuals asking these questions, they've already missed the boat. They have already complete-

*It takes more than a great suit to get a great job.*

ly given up the chance to do the things that will truly set them apart from and put them above the crowd. The things they are contemplating have <u>very</u> little impact on the interviewer's decision making process. He or she couldn't care less whether you spent $200 or $600 on your interview suit or whether your tie is striped or patterned (as long as you are clean and presentable)!

No matter what your job will be, your employer will be looking for a well-rounded individual with strengths in several key areas. It takes years of focus on them, not a few weeks or months, to be able to develop them. They are the pillars that future success will be built upon. They are the "Winning Characteristics."

# And, THEY ARE the DIFFERENCE BETWEEN SUCCESS AND FAILURE
## in the interview process.

# Career

## Chapter 6

# COMMONALITIES

*Y*ou may question whether or not the "Winning Characteristics" apply to <u>you</u>. You may be interested in a new job in a new field that didn't even exist five years ago. How could they apply?

Well, they do.

When you boil it down, whether you are in a new field or old, whether you are a computer software designer, an engineer, a physical therapist, or an accountant, you have the same job. Your goal (and responsibility) is to <u>solve problems</u> and <u>satisfy customers</u>.

Think about it.

There is no career where these two fundamental issues are not at the forefront of what you will do. Sure, the problems may present themselves in very different ways. They could be anything from a deteriorating bridge in need of stabilization to a puppy with a broken leg. Regardless of the specifics, <u>you</u> will be the person with the ability and desire to solve the problem, thereby satisfying your customer.

And your customers will come in all shapes and sizes. In a way, even your boss and your fellow workers will be your customers. They just happen to be "internal customers." They work for the same organization as you do, but to be successful you need to make them as happy as traditional customers outside of the company.

More obvious customers would be people who would purchase an automobile you help design. Regardless, if you like what you're doing (and want to continue to get paid for it), you will be in the business of satisfying customers.

Even if you have zero interest in "business" or the thought of a "traditional" career path makes you cringe, you'll still be entering a job where you'll need to solve problems and/or satisfy customers.

OUR CUSTOMERS

Let's say, for instance, you'd like to spend your life teaching kindergarten to underprivileged youth. You'll still have a number of "customers" you'll need to satisfy. They include the principal, the superintendent of schools, and probably, the school board. And, let's not forget the students or their very interested parents. In a sense, they're all customers. Hopefully, you'll help solve some of their problems and satisfy them in the process!

So, as unique as different career choices may be, there are commonalities that make them all the same.

Enter the "Winning Characteristics."

As I mentioned in the Building Your Future chapter, they are the traits your future employer or grad school will be looking for – regardless of your chosen field. The Winning Characteristics will be the key to showing that you've got what it takes to solve problems and satisfy customers.

*Let's take a* **CLOSER LOOK** *at them.*

# Chapter 7

*What your future*

# EMPLOYER IS LOOKING FOR

*Y*ou will sink or swim based on the Winning Characteristics. They may be called different things in different fields, but they are the pillars of success in <u>every</u> field.

And importantly, I'm not talking about being able to look into the interviewer's eyes and say, "Yes, I have them." I'm talking about being able to give concrete examples of when and how you have exhibited them.

So, what are these elusive Winning Characteristics?

I'll break them into seven key areas, built around the word **COLLEGE**.

**C**ommunication Skills
**O**rganizational Skills
**L**eadership
**L**ogic
**E**ffort
**G**roup Skills
**E**ntrepreneurship

# COMMUNICATION SKILLS

To be effective, you have to be able to exchange information with other people. Concise, complete delivery of an idea or problem is a fundamental skill which you'll need to master. The ability to effectively listen is equally challenging and important (more on that later).

And, given the fast pace of business today, oral communication skills are growing in importance relative to written skills. You will still need strong fundamental writing skills. But, managers today just don't have the luxury of having time to compose five page documents to help make decisions.

When they do compose documents, today's professionals tend to create them on their personal computers and send them via email. If you're getting the hint that computer skills are important, you're correct. You just won't compete well in any field without them.

Simply put, individuals who can communicate in a concise, well organized fashion (both verbally and in writing) will be strongly favored in today's environment.

# ORGANIZATIONAL SKILLS

You not only have to be able to walk and chew gum at the same time, you need to be able to juggle while you do it. It's complicated out there, and you have to be able to master the complexity.

To do so, strong organizational skills are a must. To effectively participate in a wide variety of tasks will require that you can keep track of yourself, your schedule, your files, and any number of other things you may need to in a given field. You need to be able to prioritize, focusing on important projects, managing details, and developing step by step plans to accomplish your goals.

Sure, you may have assistants and computers to help you manage the day-to-day process, but an organized thought process and the ability to keep your head above water on multiple projects at one time is of keen interest to employers.

And finally, it will be important to be able to maximize your results through smart use of resources available to you. You need to be organized to improve not only your productivity, but that of your staff and fellow team members.

## LEADERSHIP

Employers want people who will be able to come in and make a difference. They want employees who can rally a team behind them and make things happen, people who can and will take the organization in new directions.

Now, don't let this one intimidate you. Nobody is expecting you to come in and run the company overnight. They just want people who, once they're in and understand the organization, will actively work to improve it and have the ability to come up with new ideas and turn them into reality.

A central principle of management today is "empowering" employees, giving them the freedom and flexibility to make a personal difference rather than managing them closely with no room for personal judgement. Obviously, within this empowerment concept, employees who are leaders rather than simply followers are in high demand. Let me also mention that inherent in leadership is being able to get others focused with you on a goal and working together to make it a reality. Both motivating other team members and actually producing results are important parts of successful leadership.

# Logic

This is not as simple or fundamental as it sounds. Some jobs require strong analytical ability. Others require creative thinking skills. Still others require long term strategic planning or complex problem solving ability. Regardless, raw smarts and the ability to think your way to a solution play a key role in the hiring decision. By the way, these are not always the easiest qualities to be able to identify in an interview.

Clearly your G.P.A. will play a role in a recruiter's evaluation of your ability here, as will the perceived quality of your school. If the company is interviewing at your school, it obviously has some faith in the institution itself.

Your logic will also be judged based on the quality of your answers to questions in the interview. Are you well organized in your thoughts and concise and complete in your answers, or do you ramble on or never completely answer the question? It does make a difference.

# Effort

When the going gets tough, employers want someone who will rise to the challenge, not run from it. They want someone who will be willing to go the extra mile and make the personal sacrifice to get the job done correctly and on time. And, employers know a job is a marathon, not a sprint. They want individuals who can stay focused and perform consistently for the organization over an extended period of time.

It is very easy to sit in an interview and say that you are hard working and will put forth any level of effort necessary to get the desired results. It is equally easy for the interviewer not to believe you. A question like "What is the most difficult situation you have ever been in, and how did you work through it?" will help the interviewer get at this one.

What you have done during your college career will <u>prove</u> that you have the motivation and drive that is so important to them.

# GROUP SKILLS

The team approach to managing a business is definitely today's management style of choice. The smart but abrasive employee with a dominating style just doesn't do as well as he was able to even 10 years ago. Other team members won't give him cooperation or 100% effort. Therefore, more than ever, the ability to work effectively with others is critical to success.

And, this doesn't necessarily mean leading a team. It also means being an effective, contributing, non-leading team member when the situation calls for it. Yes, you not only need to know how to lead, you have to be able to follow. Once again, your personal examples will speak louder than your words.

Between the quality of your resumé and your responses during the interview, the prospective employer will walk away with a pretty good grasp of your skills in this area.

# ENTREPRENEURSHIP

The rate of change in the world is accelerating dramatically. Doing things "like we've always done them" is no longer something to be proud of in today's workplace. Unless you're selling something as antique, old, classic, or nostalgic, doing something "like we've always done it" means someone else is probably doing it faster, better, or more cost effectively.

The ability to accept and adapt to change, and the ability to <u>create</u> it are valued commodities in today's workplace. Too many employees today resist change because they are comfortable with the old way. The new way involves risk — risk of failure and extra work — which may or may not pay off depending on whether or not the new way is truly a step forward.

Here again, prospective employers are looking for real-life, concrete examples of your ability to do this. It can be things you did related to your summer job at the ice cream parlor or your sorority's intramural soccer team, but they want to know you changed something other than the channel of your TV set watching afternoon soap operas between classes.

In a nutshell, that's what they're looking for — the Winning Characteristics. The trick is to prove in concrete ways that you have developed these Winning Characteristics during your college career. And I'm not talking about just one example of how you have exhibited each characteristic. You'll want a variety of examples from different activities in different aspects of your life to prove that you have each of the seven.

Remember the acronym **COLLEGE**.

Now, before you get overwhelmed, get a headache, or give up before you even start, let me assure you of one thing. You can accomplish all these things and have a truly great time while you're in college. It's not as difficult and complex as you may think. Your academic experience, extracurricular activities, and employment environments are all loaded with opportunities.

You'll accumulate some examples of how you've exhibited the Winning Characteristics without even trying. You can get many more with some focus on it. And amazingly, some of the activities you'll get involved in to accomplish this will actually add greatly to the amount of fun you'll have in school.

*So now* **YOU KNOW.**

# Chapter 8

# *What Your*

# GRAD SCHOOL IS LOOKING FOR

**Medical school?**

**Law school?**

**Business school?**

*Y*ou may have absolutely no idea what you plan to do after graduating from college. You may not have the slightest clue as to whether or not you'll continue your formal education. Or, you may <u>know</u> that you'll be continuing your education after receiving an undergraduate degree and that you won't be interviewing for your first job for at least 6 years. Given these possible scenarios, you may wonder if this book will apply to your life.

Regardless of your path, you still have a high hurdle to jump after undergraduate graduation. It may not be an employer, but you're going to have to impress <u>somebody</u>. You need a little more going for you than a heartbeat and a thick wallet to get accepted into a top graduate school program. And, while it may surprise you, the "judges" there do think a lot like the employers discussed in the last chapter.

Are the Stanford University School of Medicine and a New York Ad Agency looking for <u>all</u> the same things in a candidate? Of course not, but the Winning Characteristics <u>are</u> commonly desired by these two dramatically different organizations.

Your possession of the Winning Characteristics will be of universal interest to any type of selection committee or interview team you'll face. They'll be the criteria used by the folks deciding if you will have the opportunity to be a part of their group, team, firm, practice, school, or company.

The days of a strong grade point average being enough to get you into any grad school are behind us. Even if it worked for a parent, relative or neighbor in the past, I promise, it will not work for you. The world has changed, and so have the criteria for excelling in it.

*Let's* **MOVE ON.**

# *Some Basics*

$T$ime for some cliches.

"You have to crawl before you can walk."

"You have to walk before you can run."

You get the idea.

The morsel of truth in these is that you do have to master some basic skills before you can move on to the more advanced ones. And, since mastering the Winning Characteristics are a bit more challenging than learning to ride a bike, the principle applies here as well.

> *You have to master some basic skills before moving on to more advanced ones.*

Just a few more cliches.

"All work and no play makes Jack a dull boy." (All play and no work makes Jack a dropout, by the way.)

"Everybody pays their dues."

"There's no free lunch."

Simply put, your willingness to manage work versus play and your commitment to "paying your dues" to make college work for you are essential to having a shot at success in college. And, the ability to master the basics of goal setting and time management will be critical. A lot of your ability to prove that you possess the Winning Characteristics will come from time utilized <u>beyond</u> the hours it will take to get adequate grades.

And, the most fundamental of fundamentals is survival. Good <u>and</u> bad, freshman year is dramatically different from anything you've ever experienced. Realistic goal setting, good time management, and the right mind-set will go a long way in ensuring you'll accomplish the "survival" fundamental.

# IF YOU DON'T GET PAST YOUR FIRST YEAR, there's not much else to concern yourself with in this book.

# Chapter 9

# *Work*

# VERSUS PLAY

*C*ollege is a great time. It's a lot of fun. There's no doubt about it. But in spite of popular theory, there really is life after college. And, it can be pretty awesome too.

The bad news is that you do have to work for a living after you graduate. The good news is that the job can be a whole lot more enjoyable to you than flipping burgers. In fact, if you do what it takes to land your dream job coming out of college, you'll probably even <u>enjoy</u> work.

And, while you'll definitely have less free time than in college, you'll have some money in your pocket to pursue your hobbies and interests, be able to afford to go to professional sports and entertainment events, and travel to some interesting places. In fact, even if you were fortunate enough to have some money in your pocket during college, it's nice to be able to spend your own money after graduation and be responsible to no one but yourself.

My point is that you don't have to try to have every bit of fun you will have in your entire life in this four year period. Take advantage of the opportunities to enjoy your time in school. There are lots of them and you should make the most of it. Have fun! Just don't go so crazy doing it that you severely damage your ability to have fun <u>after</u> school.

Remember the Cold Hard Facts?

If you don't do what you need to in college to get the job done, you could easily (and probably will) join the ranks of the almost one in two who don't graduate. Or, you could be a part of the one out of three students who will graduate between now and 2005 and will take jobs for which they don't need a college degree.

This would not be an optimal situation. Not for your career, not for your ego, and not for your bank account.

Said another way, having to work two part-time jobs as a waiter or a waitress after college to pay off your student loans would not classify as a big win by most standards. It would, on the other hand, be a potential indicator that you may have been a <u>bit</u> too focused on fun during your days in school. Balance is the key.

Let me share with you one other thought, one that is not particularly popular in some circles today. Nobody owes you anything. Not one thing. You get what you earn. Nothing more. Nothing less.

It is popular today to believe that there's a good living to be made by everyone and that the government and big corporations will take care of you. This is simply not true. I'm sorry to be the bearer of bad news, but the sooner you have this revelation, the better off you'll be.

The true reality is that you'll be graduating into a job market that is more complex and competitive than ever before. Many big companies are downsizing and tens of millions of "baby boomers" are currently camping out in the jobs you will want.

The good news is that it's still America, the "Land of Opportunity." It sounds a little "mom and dad-ish" to say it, but there still _are_ opportunities out there. Really. They may not be as obvious or as plentiful as you or I would like, but they _do_ exist. You've just got to work hard and go after them.

*The choice of whether or not*
*to* **WORK HARD** *is yours.*

# Chapter 10

## *Paying* YOUR DUES

*I*t's an old expression..."Everybody pays their dues." It's how you get ahead. And you know what? It's true. And the sooner in life you start paying, the lesser the dues you'll ultimately pay to reach a given level of achievement. Underline it, highlight it, memorize it, or write it on your wall. To get ahead, you <u>must</u> pay your dues. And the sooner you do, the lower the toll! Remember, there is no free ride.

Think of "dues paying" as an opportunity, not a task. It is a chance, through hard work, to propel yourself to a different level. <u>If</u> you choose to do it, the results will be amazing.

As I mentioned, I was informed quite clearly at my high school senior class awards assembly that I had not paid

*After college, dues paying will not be fun.*

my dues. I was not the recipient of one of the many scholarships awarded. Having an unspectacular grade point average and almost no extracurricular activities, I just wasn't one of those "ideal students" that every college was looking to throw money at to get them to attend.

The decision I made that day, to pay my dues in college and do whatever it took to stand out, was the smartest decision I've made in my life. I didn't realize it at the time, but college is the best time in life to pay your dues. The environment is so great and you have so much time on your hands that you can do it and still have a great time. The same opportunity is much less likely after college.

It is important to mention, though, that if you do not make the personal decision to pay your dues in college, your life will not end. You will, however, have a steep hill to climb after graduation to catch up to the people who did. Unfortunately, it will almost certainly include taking a job or two for which a degree is not required.

I've watched friends admirably try to play "catch up" after college, but it did not happen easily, did not happen quickly, and did not happen without great personal sacrifice.

This "dues paying" job after college will not necessarily be a great deal of fun and will most likely require night and weekend work. And, you'll need to truly excel in that position to prove to your next interviewer that you've grown up and become a more mature, responsible person since your "blow off" days in college.

One more point. Don't count on your manager at this job to be supportive or particularly helpful in your endeavors. He may or may not be a decent manager, may or may not have a college degree, may or may not like people with college degrees, and may be intimidated and feel that you're a threat to him. You just don't know.

I know this is a worst case, nightmare scenario. It's also not completely unrealistic either. Hopefully, you get the idea. It is much easier to pay your dues in college than afterwards!

*Enough preaching.*
# LET'S GO TO WORK

# SOME GOALS

*"I*t's a dream until you write it down. Then it's a goal."

GOALS

There is very little that is as simple or powerful as sitting down and writing out your goals. It sounds so easy that it seems almost silly. "Who would do it?" and "Why bother?" are obvious questions that come to mind.

Well, you're going to have to trust me (at least a little bit) on this one. It <u>can</u> be incredibly powerful if you do it with at least some degree of sincerity and then post the list in a place where you'll see it on a regular basis.

There are three parts to the process. I've just touched on steps two and three. They are the easy parts.

2. Write them down

3. Keep them in a place where you can't help but see them regularly

Step one is the bear. It goes as follows:

1. Set the Goals

To accomplish this, you need to have some feel for what you want in the short and long term.

It's better to start by looking out into the distant future. Where do you want to be in 10 years? More specifically, where do you want to be personally and professionally at that point. Even if you don't yet have a feel for what career direction you'd like to pursue, you certainly should be able to put together a mental picture of what type of lifestyle you'd like to have at that point in your life.

## A 10 Year Look

Answering the following questions may help:

· Where will you live? _____

· What type of home/apartment will you have? _____

_____

· What will you do for fun? _____

_____

· Who will your friends be? _____

_____

· What kind of clothes will you wear? _____

_____

· Will you be single or married? (Obviously someone else gets to vote on this one, too.) _____

· What kind of physical condition will you be in? How will you accomplish this? _____

_____

· What type of career might you have to support this lifestyle? __

_____

· How serious will you be about your career? _____

_____

Two hints here.

First, the lifestyle you want is probably significantly more expensive than you would imagine. Second, life is a building process (see Chapter 10 - Paying Your Dues). You probably won't go from a job flippin' burgers to a $50,000 a year career overnight. You'll need to be a little realistic in thinking about where you want to be.

You hopefully now have a better vision of where you'd like to be long term. You'll set some short term goals to help you get there later in the book.

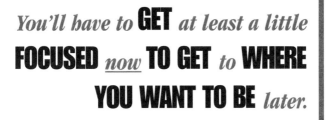

*You'll have to* **GET** *at least a little* **FOCUSED** *now* **TO GET** *to* **WHERE YOU WANT TO BE** *later.*

# Chapter 12

# Managing

# YOUR TIME

*T*ime Management. It sounds <u>boring</u>, but it's critical to making the most of your college experience. Hopefully, you'll set some aggressive goals for yourself. Time management will help you achieve them.

As a starting point, you need to realize that you have a lot of time on your hands in college. "A lot" probably doesn't even do it justice. An "unbelievable amount" may be more appropriate. If you get eight hours of sleep a night (fat chance!), that will give you 16 hours a day to work with! If you get a more typical six hours, you'll have 18 hours a day to work with. That's a tremendous amount of time.

Not to get overly technical, but 18 hours a day is 126 hours a week. If you're taking a typical 16 hours a week of classes, that leaves 110 hours to study, pursue extracurricular activities, have ridiculous amounts of fun, and take care of life's necessities (like eating, laundry, etc.). Even if you decide that every Wednesday, Thursday, Friday, and Saturday from 6 p.m. on will be fully dedicated to the concept of fun, you still have almost 80 hours left. In most cases (if you don't have a job while school is in session), you'll have more time on your hands than you ever have before or ever will again.

Some thoughts on how to manage it.

First, schedule early classes — Eight o'clock classes if you can get up easily, nine o'clock if you can't. They will force you to get out of bed at a reasonable time, not unlike you did in high school (or what your future employer will expect from you). You'd be <u>amazed</u> at how easy it is to sleep 'til 10:30 if your first class starts at 11:00.

And when you schedule these early classes, you have to go to them! Know yourself. If you can't consistently make 8:00 classes (although you really ought to be able to), go for 9:00's. Even I could make it to 9:00's. You can too.

Second, study between classes. Often you'll have one or two hours to kill. Go to the library and put those hours to work for you. It's amazing the number of ways that people waste time between classes. Get into the routine of making some valuable use out of these time slots. It's not that tough. And realistically, there aren't that many better things you can be doing from 10:00 a.m. to noon on a Tuesday morning.

Third, study after class before dinner. This seems rather obvious, but you'd be blown away at how many college students watch soap operas, Jerry Springer, and reruns of The Simpsons in the afternoon. It's incredible. They'll sit there for hours a day for weeks at a time. Spending hours on-line in chat rooms and playing computer games are also a way of life for some of today's "high tech" students. But last time I checked, these options were not that "fun" anyway, so why not put this time to better use and have some real fun in the evening or on the weekend.

By the way, studying in front of the TV – trying to have fun <u>and</u> study all at once – does not make you a time management wizard. You'll get little or nothing from the studying and miss about half of the show. It's the epitome of bad time management.

***Big time waster, bad idea***

Fourth, when you study, focus on it. Make it quality study time, not social time. Do it in a quiet environment and at a high level of intensity. Personally, I wouldn't even listen to music unless it's purely instrumental (no lyrics), and you're doing it to drown out some background noise. If you maximize the quality of the effort, you'll <u>minimize</u> the amount of time you need to give it. More on that later.

In general, make the most of your days. The temptations not to study are fewer and much less exciting during the day and it will free up your evenings for extracurriculars and more legitimate fun.

If you take 16 hours a week of classes starting at 9:00 a.m. each day, take an hour lunch, go to the library between and after classes and finish at 5:00 p.m., you'll have put in 19 hours at the library in a week. That is a <u>tremendous</u> amount of study time on a week-in week-out basis. Your nights and weekends will be totally free (other than before midterms or finals) and you'll have a serious head start towards a strong grade point average. Sounds pretty manageable, doesn't it?

Looking at the bigger picture, you should manage your time from a total semester standpoint. Get or create some type of good daily

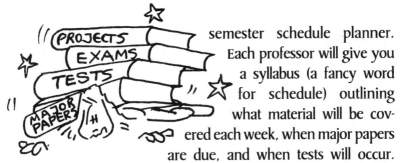

semester schedule planner. Each professor will give you a syllabus (a fancy word for schedule) outlining what material will be covered each week, when major papers are due, and when tests will occur. Write them all down on one calendar so you'll know when your biggest "crunch times" will take place. Knowing in advance will allow you to get a head start on some of the work to avoid getting "burned" during those time frames.

Before I end this section, let me throw out a thought about holding down a job while in school. If you need to work while school is in session to be able to afford to do things like pay tuition and eat, take everything I've said about the importance of time management and multiply it by three. Your task is significantly more difficult. But it is still workable if you realize and act like your single most precious commodity is time. You just can't waste it.

If you work during the day, you'll need to schedule study hours around your job, including time at night <u>and</u> on weekends. You need to "show up" to study as diligently as you "show up" to work. It will require a lot of the dreaded "d" word — discipline — but there's no other way to effectively master this challenging situation. You'll find an entire chapter on working during college later in this book.

*College is great.*
# MAKE THE MOST OF EVERY MINUTE.

# Chapter 13

*Surviving*

# YEAR ONE

*I*f "surviving" is not on your list of freshman goals, perhaps you should reconsider. Last year, almost three in 10 freshmen did not achieve this goal and did not return as sophomores. That's a <u>big</u> number, and a <u>huge</u> waste of time and money.

In my freshman corridor, our Resident Assistant (an upperclassmen who is paid to live in a freshman dorm to keep order and provide student-to-student perspective) called us together during our first week. He told the 40 of us to look around. He said that five of us would probably not make it to second semester and that 10 of us would not make it to sophomore year. I thought he was just trying to scare us. He wasn't.

Six guys weren't back for second semester. A full dozen never saw their sophomore year. These guys were not stupid. In fact, most of them were pretty bright. They just lacked balance. I'll share with you the story of two of them to make the point. I have not changed the names (at least not the nicknames) to protect the innocent. The stories and the people are real.

The guys were Spaceman and Worm (18 year old guys can come up with some weird nicknames). Both went to way more than their share of parties and had several years worth of fun during their first semester. Worm stayed out late, slept in late, and played a whole lot of hoops. The Spaceman stayed out late, got up early, and disappeared during the afternoon. Worm flunked out. Spaceman made the Dean's list.

What was the difference? Spaceman went to class. We also found out later that he spent his afternoons at the library. There was <u>no</u> shortage of college fun in his life. He just had a little bit of balance.

There was one other common feature of all the "one semester wonders" I knew. They dug themselves an incredible hole in the first six weeks. They didn't go to class regularly. They didn't do their assignments. They didn't do the necessary reading. They thought they could catch up later "like they did in high school." The hole they dug was so deep that it was close to impossible to get out. And they didn't.

Make a commitment to survive the first year. Start by not getting buried your first six weeks. Be a "geek." Read your assignments <u>before</u> the class. Do your homework problems twice. Go to <u>every</u> class. Overstudy for quizzes and tests. Survive the first six weeks and then go for the whole semester and the whole year. You do have to do some serious work to handle a college course load, but you'll learn how to do it effectively if you make the effort.

Also worth mentioning is that a reasonable course load will help. And, don't be afraid to put an easy course on the list. It can help you keep your head above water while you're battling a killer calculus or chemistry class.

Let's for a minute get a little loftier with our goals. Let's talk about not just "surviving" your freshman year. Let's talk about actually doing well. <u>Somebody</u> has to get the A's and B's. It might as well be you. Beyond being allowed to come back for a second year, there are a number of other advantages to getting off to a fast start.

First, once you get some decent grades, you'll know you're capable of more. You'll get a bit more comfortable with the idea of success in college and settle in quickly toward making it a reality.

Second, it will open doors to some significant opportunities. From student government to the campus newspaper, the groups you want to join will want <u>you</u> to join <u>them</u>. If they think you can barely handle your current course load, they will not think you'll be able to make a meaningful contribution to their group.

They may tell you that grades do not play a big role in their decision-making process. They'll do that right up to the moment when they instead opt for candidates who already have a grasp on their academic challenges. That's a fancy way of saying that people with good grades are going to get the spots you want. As we'll discuss later, these extracurriculars will be <u>critical</u> to your interviewing success.

Let's also look at how you'll help your future employment cause with good first year grades. When you start interviewing for internships your junior year, you'll have only two years of grades in your cumulative average. When you do your initial resumé as a senior, you'll only have three years behind you. Your freshman grades will have a <u>tremendous</u> impact on these numbers.

If they are good grades, they will pull the cumulative average up. On the other hand, if you get a 2.0, even a strong 3.5 your sophomore year will leave you with a 2.75 going into internship interviews. If you follow with a respectable 3.2 your junior year, you'll still only have a 2.9. Had you rallied to a 3.0 your freshman year, you'd be in good shape with a cumulative 3.2 with the 3.5 sophomore and 3.2 junior performance mentioned above. A strong freshman performance can be a big help.

A solid freshman year academic performance can pay many positive dividends for you. So make a commitment to success in the first six weeks, then in the first semester, and do your best from there.

*And remember,*

# PLAYING "CATCH UP" *is*
# NOT AN OPTION

*at the college level.*

# Section V

## Getting the Grades

$T$o ensure you will get a great career opportunity coming out of college, this is where it begins. No, getting good grades alone will not convince potential employers that you have <u>all</u> of the Winning Characteristics they are looking for.

It will, however, let them know that you have some mix of **Logic** and **Organizational Skills**. It will let them know you're willing to put forth **Effort** to achieve your goals. And, it will get you into the interview so you can showcase those many other strengths you do possess.

If you don't get decent grades, you're dead before you start. It will be extremely tough to get an interview for an outstanding job. And, even if you do, put yourself in the interviewer's shoes. Why should she believe that you are intelligent and mature enough to do the job for them if you haven't done your job particularly well for the past

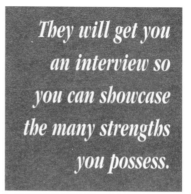

*They will get you an interview so you can showcase the many strengths you possess.*

four years? And, if you were her, would you want to go back to your boss and tell him or her that your best candidate has a 2.4 average? I don't think so.

No individual thing you'll learn in this section is the one magic thing that will make college easy. Taken as a whole, though, they can and should significantly improve your academic performance. Hopefully, you will also already have some study techniques that have worked for you during high school. If you do, work them into your college study plans. It's really all about what works for you.

Along with helping you get good grades, good study techniques can also make you more efficient so you don't have to spend your entire college life in the library.

After all, there is
# MORE TO COLLEGE THAN STUDYING.

# Chapter 14

# How good do

# YOUR GRADES HAVE TO BE?

*I* can not be too emphatic here. **YOU DO NOT NEED A 4.0 STRAIGHT "A" AVERAGE TO SUCCEED AFTER COLLEGE.** It's just not necessary to have a perfect grade point average. On the other hand, if you're not willing to work any harder than it will take to get a 2.2, don't even bother to go. With this type of performance, you will most likely not improve your career opportunities relative to a high school graduate.

With a weak academic performance, you'll be almost certain to join the crew working at Burgerama after graduation. So either plan to do better than a 2.2 or save yourself the work, time, and the money involved in going to college and get a job right out of high school.

While these are rough guidelines (and there certainly are exceptions), you can typically get a good job out of college with a 3.0 average overall and a 3.3 average in your major. You can get a great job with a 3.5 overall and a 3.5 in your major. I might point out that in a weak economy it might take numbers a bit better than these to get the job you want. In a strong economy, you may be able to get away with a bit less.

The key point here is that these numbers will get you an interview and will put the interviewer in a positive frame of mind when she meets you. They get you in the game. They alone <u>will</u> <u>not</u> get you the job. There are too many good people out there, just too much competition. As I mentioned, good grades will effectively sell your ability to think (**Logic**). They will probably also reinforce the fact that you are **Organized** and motivated to succeed (**Effort**), but that's about as far as it goes. You need to show that you have <u>all</u> of the Winning Characteristics. Three of seven will not get it done.

On the flip side, if you lack the grades, you probably won't even get an interview. And even if you do, you'll have a steep uphill battle just to get the interviewer's attention. The interviewer will talk to approximately 16 students in a given day. If you don't have the grades, you certainly are not her lead candidate going in.

If you're planning to go into a Sales or Marketing related position, you may think you don't need the grades. You'll just need to be able to sell yourself well in an interview. Wrong. These fields are now much more complex than they have been historically, and the ability to think strategically and do complex numerical analysis is more critical than ever. Again, if you can't get the grades in college, why should an employer believe you could perform in her organization? It's a competitive job market. The employer just doesn't need to take the risk.

On the opposite side of the spectrum, even if you plan to major in a numbers based field like finance or engineering, there's a lot more to getting hired these days than just grades. They're still important. They're just not the complete picture. Firms want well rounded individuals, not just people who can get a 3.96 by living in the library.

One final point. If you are a gifted individual capable of that elusive 3.96, I would suggest that you get even more focused on extracurriculars. Spend the extra time rounding yourself out. Even if your grades slip to a 3.6 or 3.7, there is no doubt about your thinking abil-

*You don't need to LIVE in the library.*

ities. You're smart! What you do with that extra time could make the difference on interview day.

If you have a 3.96 but have done nothing but study for four years, what exactly do you plan to talk about in the interview? Besides, those other activities will prove that you didn't need to spend 12 hours a day, seven days a week with your face in a book to get your grades.

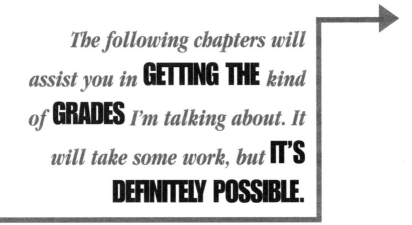

*The following chapters will assist you in* **GETTING THE** *kind of* **GRADES** *I'm talking about. It will take some work, but* **IT'S DEFINITELY POSSIBLE.**

# *Chapter 15*

# PROFESSORS

*W*ake up. This is one of the most critical chapters in the book.

Professors are people. They have personalities. They have egos. They develop relationships, and sometimes, yes, they even show compassion. They are all different, and understanding them is critical. It can be extremely beneficial to you. Don't underestimate it.

Think for a minute about what would make someone choose to become a professor. It will help you think about them in the proper light as you consider how to interact with them.

You would choose to become a professor, I think, because you had a strong interest in and knowledge of a subject area. And, because you very much enjoyed sharing that with other people, and enjoyed being around college students in a campus setting. And you would, most probably, be pretty smart.

Professors think they are experts in their subject areas.

Fortunately, most are. Unfortunately, a few aren't. Regardless, the key insight here is that a professor, believing he is an expert in his field, is going to lecture on the subject matter he thinks is most important. And, if he lectures on specific topics, he'll test on them too.

In general, professors believe they have something more important to say or a different and better way to explain it than the guy who wrote the text book they are teaching from. They may not have personally chosen the book they are teaching from and may or may not even like it. And, the bigger or more prestigious the school, the bigger the egos and the more this phenomenon exists.

*The key is probably NOT the books.*

On the other hand, if your professor wrote the book, this obviously changes things quite a bit. The book becomes the Bible. If your professor believed her thoughts were important enough to put in writing, you can bet she will lecture and test directly from her book.

Now that we've established the importance of your focus on the lecture material, it follows that you absolutely have to go to class and be attentive. I know I sound like somebody's mom or dad when I say this, but you do need to suck it up, go to class, and stay awake when you get there.

Think about it. If the professor didn't write the book, studying it astutely to make up for missing three weeks of class will be futile. It may not even cover the same material! You'll surely crash and burn. You have to go to class. And while you're in class, don't spare the ink. Take lots of notes to capture the lecture points!

If a professor says something three or four times, she obviously thinks it's important. Write it down a couple times and somehow highlight the fact that it was heavily emphasized. You <u>will</u> see it again on exam day.

Blowing off class and borrowing someone's notes isn't the answer either. If you can actually read what they wrote, can you understand what the notes mean? What was the professor's area of emphasis? What point did she repeat three times? What question did she promise would be on the test? (This happens a lot more than you would think.) Borrowing notes to make up for sleeping late just does-n't work. Believe me, I've tried it. It's definitely better than nothing, but it's just not the same as being there.

Let me share another thought related to professors' mind-sets and skipping or sleeping through class. It makes them mad. They are will-ing to share their wisdom with you by teaching. You, by not showing up physically or mentally, are telling them that you really don't care what they have to say. Not a brilliant idea.

If you are going to show up for class, try to participate. Many stu-dents, particularly in their freshman and sophomore year, think that professors are unapproachable, almost as if they are from another planet. The students are afraid that the professor will find out how little they actually know if they speak up and ask a question. They also value their fellow students' class time (more than is necessary) and don't want to waste it with a "stupid" question.

If you're confused in class, stop the train! Ask the question. You've paid a whole lot of money to be there. Do not be embarrassed to get clarification on an issue. It sounds a bit corny, but other people probably really do have the same question as you do. And since in most subjects the next point builds on the last one, once you're lost, you're just going to become more and more confused as the class progresses. So go ahead, ask the question!

Now, if you've asked several questions and just aren't getting it, let the professor proceed and go see her at "office hours," time formally set aside for helping students in need of additional assistance.

 Going to class, asking questions, and going to office hours offer other advantages. They let professors know that you care, that you're a serious student who is giving his or her best effort. It lets them know you have a genuine interest in the subject area they have chosen as their life's work. It's the students who do this that get the break if they are near the cutoff point between two grades. In many cases, grades aren't given just by the numbers. **Effort** does count.

Some additional thoughts on office hours. They are set up specifically for you to go ask questions. Take advantage of this opportunity throughout the semester. The professor sits at office hours with no visitors for weeks at a time. Then, the day before a test, half the class tries to get in to get a question answered. Obviously this doesn't always work out too well. If you have questions, go regularly. Don't wait until the day before the test!

Grade trends count, too. If your professor knows you've been giving it your all and you've had a C, a B and an A respectively on tests going into finals, you may want to try to negotiate with her before the final to give you an A for the class if you can pull an A on her cumulative final. In some cases, she'll take you up on it. Even if she doesn't, she'll remember you if you're "on the bubble" between two grades after the final.

If it's finals week and she has never seen you before (at office hours or actively participating in class), you can forget any of this type of negotiation. You're going to get what the numbers dictate.

There are other advantages to developing a positive relationship with your instructors. When it comes time to seek employment, they can be good friends to have. They tend to be fairly well connected in their fields. In fact, interviewers who are alumni of the school will often call them to find out who their top students are. Professors can also be excellent sources of letters of recommendation. These letters can give you a leg up, particularly if you want to get an interview with a company that's not coming to your school.

A final point on relationships with professors – be sincere. If you think that buddying up with professors is a license to slack off in their classes and still get decent grades, you're going to learn a painful lesson. You're not going to do well.

If you haven't been to class for months, you'll also strike out if you show up the week before finals to convince them how hard you're trying. They weren't born yesterday and will see you coming a mile away.

Before ending this chapter, I would be remiss if I didn't discuss professors with intimidating styles. They're out there and you'll most probably end up sitting in a few of their classrooms. I'll break them into two categories, the "Stretchers" and the "Breakers."

The Stretchers are great. They want to prepare you for the "real world" by teaching you as much as they possibly can. They'll put you on the spot with tough questions in class. They're generally good natured people but they'll "push" on you a bit, making you question yourself to see if you'll effectively stand up for your point of view or if you'll crumble at the first opportunity to do so.

*Good profs may stretch you a bit.*

The key for them will be to see if you can support yourself with relevant facts from the course. In their minds, your future boss is going to do it so why not give you a little experience in this area sooner as opposed to later.

They'll also make their exams extremely challenging, resulting in class averages as low as 50% or 55%. They believe that if they make you reach for the stars, that while you may not get there, you'll get a lot closer than if you had shot for a lesser goal. Fortunately, these professors understand the concept of the curve and of a normal distribution of grades (i.e., 15% of the class gets an A, 30% get a B,...). Stretchers aren't out to destroy you (or your grade point average). They're just out to make you the best you can be. Frankly, I think it's a valid philosophy.

The Breakers, on the other hand, are generally unhappy with the world and want to share that feeling with all their "lucky" students. You'll recognize this charming philosophy in the first couple weeks of their classes. They don't want to stretch you; they want to break you. They like having the power to be able to do so.

My advice is not to be combative with these types of folks. You'll lose. Just stay off their black lists and do the best that you can. Just be reassured that they can't flunk the entire class, in spite of what they tell you. The other good news is that there are very few of these folks in the business. I encountered only two of them in my four years of school. Considering that you'll have some 40 professors during four years of college, it's very manageable. You just need to know they're out there.

Understand how your professors think. Spend the time to get to know them. It is worth the effort you'll put forth doing it.

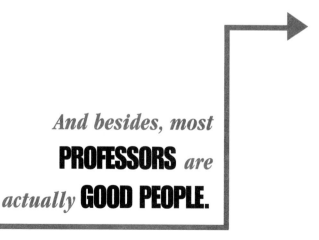

*And besides, most* **PROFESSORS** *are* *actually* **GOOD PEOPLE.**

# Chapter 1

# Class selection

# STRATEGY

*C*lass selection is something that should be done with careful thought. There are several potential strategies to follow. They will have a major impact on your grades and the learning you take away from your college experience.

BASKET WEAVING 101

EARLY BIOLOGY
TRIG. II
CALCULUS

You can pick the easiest professors or the most difficult. You can even choose the most popular, believing that if they are interesting, entertaining people, they'll better hold your interest and keep you going to class.

I suggest a combination of these strategies. I would recommend challenging professors within your major – not necessarily the ones with the reputation for flunking half the class, but the Stretchers, the teachers with a reputation for being most knowledgeable and pushing their students. Your grade point average <u>will</u> survive. A professor who is trying to truly educate you and help you grow personally has no great incentive or desire to destroy your G.P.A.

If you want to get a job related to your major after college, you'll want to actually learn something in these classes. If you don't, you're asking for trouble. Your future employer will expect you to know at least a "little bit" about what they hired you to do since you have theoretically studied the subject area for several years.

In fact, you'll probably have problems even before graduation if you try to take the easiest route early in your major. Classes in your major tend to build on each other. So if you take the easy professor in Economics 201 and 202, you may have a serious problem when you get to Economics 301 if only a tough professor is teaching the class. He won't try to reteach you what he thinks you just learned! It's more likely you'll be buried instead.

You'll obviously want to take classes required by the school and within your major on the recommended timetable, filling out your schedule with elective options based on where your interests lie. These electives (classes not specifically required) will present themselves for the most part during your junior and senior years. Which choices are right for you will be a little more clear to you at that time.

I will mention that you should look at the possibility of a minor or second major when you make class selections. In some cases you can pick up a related minor with the addition of just a few additional classes or even a second major with less work than you may anticipate. You'll get to take fewer diverse elective classes, but it will improve your marketability in your future job hunt. I'm not saying you <u>need</u> a minor or a second major, but you should at least understand what your options are.

In all required classes outside your major, I would recommend a slightly less rigorous approach. If a natural science course is a requirement (and your major or career interests have <u>nothing</u> to do with natural sciences), there is very little incentive to take the hardest class you can find. I know this is not politically correct, but fining a "manageable" science class is a good decision for you personally if you are balancing the classes with more difficult courses in your major or time consuming extracurricular activities. Remember why you are going to college in the first place.

One of the classes I took to fulfill my science requirements was Physics in Sports. It was <u>very</u> "manageable," allowed me to focus on classes that were more meaningful to my career direction, and had no negative effect on my grade point average (I got an A!).

***This is all the Physics you probably need.***

After you get through your course requirements outside your major, electives are also good candidates for "manageable" classes. A warning here, though. Do not take a class you have absolutely no interest in just because you have heard it's an "easy A." A good friend who loves European history may have thought a Russian Art class was a breeze. You, on the other hand, may be <u>so</u> bored that you fall asleep at your desk on a daily basis and struggle to get a "C."

An "easy A" recommendation alone is not a good enough reason to take a class you'll hate. Take electives that are of at least some interest to <u>you</u>.

I took a Nutrition class for Dietetics majors because I was genuinely interested in learning about the subject matter. It was a hard class and violated the "manageability" philosophy. I was interested in the subject matter, though, so I spent the time necessary to do well in the class. A decision to take a difficult class that will be personally rewarding to you can be a good choice. Just plan to spend time on it, or plan to hurt your G.P.A.

Related to that, don't be afraid to utilize your pass/fail option. At most schools you can take a number of classes and receive credits for them but receive no grade as long as you pass. If you do have an area outside of your major that you'd like to learn about, pass/fail represents an outstanding opportunity. You don't want the "C" you get in Wine Tasting 301 to hurt your grade point average. You'd be amazed at how many people get burned that way. The professors of those types of fun classes are working hard to legitimize them. If they don't, at some point the classes will be eliminated − and their jobs with them. They have no credibility if they give everyone "A's."

Pass/fail is also a good strategy to pursue for a class or two outside your major during a quarter or semester when you are taking several extremely difficult and time consuming classes within your major. It helps even the load.

The best pass/fail philosophy I have found is to plan to ace the tests during the term and slide by on the final. If you get off to a strong start and get a couple of "A's" or "B's," you'll need to spend no more than an hour or two studying for the final − when your time is of tremendous value to you.

Another important point. If you desperately want or need to get into a class and go to registration only to find it full or "closed," don't give up. Sign up for an alternate class as a fall back. Then go talk to the professor of the class you want and tell him you really want to take his class.

If this does not work, go to his class. After three or four class sessions and repeated begging on your part, most professors will let you in. Other students will drop the class or the professor will just make room for one more. This will work most of the time. But, do register for and attend the other class until you are successful. After you are, you can drop the alternate. Just don't get caught a class short!

Another important part of good class selection strategy will be effective professor selection. How do you know which professors will best fit _your_ strategy? Good question. You won't right away. But over time, by talking to fellow classmates and upperclassmen, you'll get a sense of direction here. Upperclassmen with the same or a similar major are good prospects. They will have recently completed courses you need to take and have excellent "real life" experience with these professors. Key to mention is that you want to ask students who are doing well in their classes. Arguably, their advice is a bit more credible.

Another helpful thing is the fact that a professor often teaches a number of different classes. If you like her for one (and do well), take her for another. It sounds simple, but it will be one less new teacher you will need to understand in a given semester.

One last point about professors. Fame is not an effective measure of teaching ability. The skills required to engineer a breakthrough scientific finding or a new financial theory are in fact very different from those required to effectively teach a class of 500. Even if the professor is highly acclaimed, ask some upperclassmen in your major what kind of experience they have had with him before signing up for his course.

Picking the right professors can be a tremendous advantage in any major at any school. Put it to work for you.

### _It_ WILL MAKE _a_ DIFFERENCE.

# *Listening*

# *Chapter 17*

# UP

*B*arring any physical limitations, we can all listen, right? Wrong, we can all <u>hear</u>. A bit like seeing, hearing is not something we spend a whole lot of time working at. It just kind of happens. Not so with listening.

And, the ability (or lack of it) to truly listen and absorb information will have a major impact on your ability to excel in all aspects of your college career. It's also an important half of the **Communication Skills** equation – a half you'll definitely need to impress an employer.

It is quite interesting to think about the difference in the level of training we receive in the areas of reading, writing, speaking, and listening. Of the four, we probably read or write the least. Between school, social and family conversation, TV, radio, movies, etc., we probably listen the most. Yet, we receive little or no training in listening skills. On the other hand, reading and writing are major parts of our educational system.

Listening should be active, not passive. To do it well, you need the right environment <u>and</u> attitude. Some specific steps you can take are as follows:

- Create proximity. Sit up front. While this is not a popular thought, it forces you to be attentive. Even if the subject material that day is a bit dry, common courtesy will keep you from snoozing if you're 10 to 15 feet from the lecturer. If you're in the last two or three rows, there's nothing to stop you from catching a few Z's and missing out on critical test material.

- Sit at attention. Lean forward, not against your seat back. Good, upright posture will help you stay mentally "in the game."

- Avoid distractions. Sit in a seat with a view of nothing interesting but the professor. Generally speaking, window view seats are a losing proposition. Sitting up front also helps you block out distractions.

- Focus intensely. Think about and attempt to understand what the professor is telling you. Work at it.

- Put your pen to work. Make the effort to record <u>all</u> new ideas and facts you are taught during the class.

- Ask questions. Nothing promotes poor listening like a fundamental lack of understanding.

One challenge in listening effectively is to fill what is called the "thought speed" gap. Simply put, you are able to process information a lot faster than the professor can deliver it.

In theory, you can think independently at a rate of over 600 words per minute. A normal person will lecture at about 125 words per minute, leaving your mind a whole lot of spare time to wander to <u>anything</u> but the subject at hand.

The thought speed gap doesn't necessarily mean you have to be bored. You can utilize this excess capacity to make sure you <u>truly</u>

understand what the teacher is lecturing on and that your notes are meticulous. But you have to work at it. If you catch yourself day-dreaming, quickly refocus and get back in the game. The more you practice this, the better you'll get at it.

And finally, plan to get a little bit mentally fatigued by the end of class. Active listening does take energy and will wear you down. The good news, though, is that it will have a <u>major</u> positive impact on your academic performance.

*I hope you're* **LISTENING.**

# Chapter 18

# "Notes-notes"

# AND OTHER STUDY SECRETS

*S*tudying is easy. It just takes time. Right? It is if your goal is only to pass. If you're looking for a B or better, a slightly more sophisticated approach is in order.

As I mentioned, most professors lecture on the subject matter they believe is most important. It follows from this that they will test on those same areas. Therefore, I can not overemphasize the importance of knowing the material in your notes.

Let me explain what I mean when I say "know the material." Knowing means absorbing and understanding, not just memorizing. This is the major difference in college tests versus most you've had in high school. In high school, if you were able to memorize a list of things and write them down on the test, you were in great shape. You didn't have to have any idea what lists meant, you just needed to scribble them on paper. In college, if you don't truly understand the material, you'll get tripped up on the test. College exams are intentionally designed to reward thinkers, not memorizers.

I stumbled onto an interesting concept in high school that was the basis for a great deal of my academic success in college. My chemistry teacher, who was probably the best and most demanding high school teacher I had, covered a tremendous amount of material in his classes and expected us to know it all — in detail. To give us a fair chance, he let us bring a 3 x 5 index card into our tests with anything we wanted written on both sides of it. He actually <u>invited</u> us to bring "cheat sheets" to the test.

What I would do to prepare for these tests, of course, was scour my notes to try to figure out what was most important and most difficult in them. From there, I would transfer these points onto notebook paper and see if I had too much, too little, or just enough material to fit on my "cheat sheet." I always had too much so I would have to pick out the most difficult and most important concepts from these condensed notes and write them on my index cards in the smallest print possible with the finest point pen I could find. Believe it or not, I took the index cards into the test but never needed to use them. In the process of deciding what the most important and difficult concepts were, I accidentally learned them!

Hence the concept of "notes-notes."

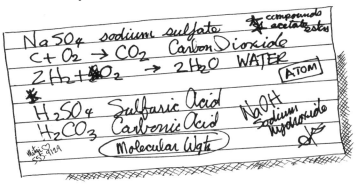

***Notes-notes' could be the secret to your success.***

Review your notes once thoroughly and make separate notes of the material that you think is most critical and was most heavily emphasized. It will be things like key formulas, principles, or lists of things. You'll boil 50 to 60 pages of notes into 5 or 6 pages of true focus points. These new notes are your "notes-notes." You need to memorize them, understand them, and be able to apply them to hit the jackpot on the exam.

Just using a highlighter on your old notes is not a good shortcut and I'd strongly recommend against it. The exercise of writing them down doesn't take that long and does actually help you learn the material.

Once you spend some time learning these "notes-notes," really focusing on them, you'll have the fundamentals for success on the exam. After you review them intensively several times and understand them, then you can go back through your main notes and pick up the rest of the details. Even if you run out of time to study, you'll still be knowledgeable in the most critical areas. You'll be amazed at how far this will get you on a test.

Conversely, you can slowly plod through the notes, memorizing every word on every page with no emphasis on focus points. If you run out of time, you'll never grasp the "big picture" of what the professor is trying to teach you. You won't be able to reason your way to answers based on your understanding of the key points. You'll just be able to spit out what you memorized, and you'll get hammered on the test – a far inferior approach and result relative to using "notes-notes."

Another outstanding reason for taking "notes-notes" is that for cumulative finals, you'll have a much easier time relearning the key lecture points from early in the semester. It's a lot more efficient to review 10 or 12 pages of "notes-notes" from two previous tests than starting over with 150 pages of old notes to relearn. And, since the most important information from those test periods is in your "notes-notes" anyway, it's an excellent place to start. You'll have four or five finals in a one week period, so this advantage can be <u>tremendous</u>.

One minor hint here. If you bombed either of the two earlier tests during the semester/quarter, you need to decide if you did a lousy job taking "notes-notes" or just didn't truly learn the material in them. If you did a lousy job on the "notes-notes," do them over.

Other good things to include in your "notes-notes" are points that the professor strongly hints will be on the test. During class when he says something like "This is something that you would be well served not to forget," circle it, star it, and capitalize it. Some professors will flat-out tell you that something will be covered on the test. They're not trying to give the test away. They just think the piece of information or formula is so important that they want you to intensely study it and attempt to truly understand it.

Do whatever is necessary to highlight the focus point in your notes — but plan to put it in your "notes-notes" and plan to know it. I was always <u>amazed</u> at the number of people who would completely ignore the hints and do nothing to their notes to make these points stand out. If the professor suggests that something may be on the test, there's a 98% chance it will be!

If the class is a numbers based class (i.e., Accounting, Calculus, etc.) or any type of problem solving class, rework the homework problems as a means of studying. Do not just look at the previous work you've done and follow through the thought process. Shut the book and do it from scratch. It's a more active form of studying and will lead to greater retention. Most problems you'll see on the test will have some similarity to homework problems you've previously been assigned. Truly understanding how to solve them will put you in a strong position on test day.

Note that with both note review and problem solving, I'm recommending an active approach rather than a passive one.

DO SOMETHING — don't just rock on a library chair staring blindly at ink on a page.

***Get active and DO something!***

You may know that a different approach than we've discussed here works best for you. Great! You're the one who needs to ace the test. But some type of active "DO SOMETHING" approach is almost always the best choice.

I suppose I would be a bit remiss if I didn't mention textbooks in a chapter on studying. While you probably can't ignore them completely. do not make them the primary focus of your efforts. If you can find out that test material will come only from the notes (and it will with over half of your classes), you may be able to spend a whole lot less time and effort reviewing book highlights.

How will you know? You'll know one of two ways. First, you'll ask. There's nothing wrong with, on a one-on-one basis, asking a professor the question, "If I've taken excellent lecture notes and know everything in them, can I get an A on this test?" Professors will answer this question honestly, particularly if you do it when 399 other people aren't listening. (They may answer a bit more "by the book" with the big group tuned in). If the answer is yes, follow their lead.

The other way you'll figure out that you can save some time and minimize focus on the text book is your personal history with the teacher. If this is your second or third test in a class, it's not too tough to figure this out. You can also find out from friends who have previously had the professor for a class. This is much riskier, however, depending on the friend. Finally, you may have the same professor for different classes (like Economics 201 and 202). He will rarely use the assigned text book for 202 if he ignored it during 201.

If you do need to focus heavily on the book, try to keep up with the reading and highlight on a week-to-week basis so you don't have 200 pages to read the week of the test. In this case, you can just study your highlights. If you don't keep up (you realistically can't in <u>every</u> class), learn your "notes-notes" before getting into the book. They're more important anyway and the reading will go much faster and be more beneficial if you do. You'll already have a fundamental understanding of the material and will absorb many more of the details from the text.

One other way a textbook may come in handy is as an additional resource for clarification. Even if the professor is only testing from lecture material, the book can be a resource to eliminate confusion. If you just don't understand something the professor is saying (or can't get to her to ask a question), the book may explain it in a different way or offer an example that makes the concept come together for you.

Or, if you are a person who generally enjoys reading, go ahead and read the book for the additional perspective it may offer. But, if possible, know ahead of time if you <u>need</u> it to be successful or if it's just a nice extra to have.

I suppose I should also mention test files. If you can get your hands on tests the professor has given in the past, it can significantly help your effort. You'll get a feel for his style of testing and what material he thinks is important. Don't be your own worst enemy here though. Here are several examples of brilliant things I've seen done related to test files. To me, they seem like obvious "don'ts." But believe me, I've seen people try them and fail miserably. They are as follows:

- People spending the entire night before the test trying to run down a copy of last year's test rather than studying. Pure brilliance!

- People assuming that they have found the "holy grail" when they find the old test. Knowing that they will now ace the exam, they spend the night before it at a party. Another sensible idea!

- People not reading a question carefully on the test and therefore assuming that it is exactly the same as one last year. They then answer it incorrectly, of course. Way to go, Einstein!

Once again, professors, as a rule, did not just fall off a turnip truck. Old tests will be helpful in giving you a feel for a professor's testing style but will not be identical to your test and will not be your saving grace.

Another subject worth mentioning is studying with other people. Studying with other people can be very helpful and greatly improve your results under the right conditions. As with most other things, though, there are do's and don'ts to consider if you're going to try it.

First, study with someone as smart or smarter than you are. You don't want to spend the night before the test tutoring someone. It is extremely frustrating and leads to very poor results (for you, not them).

Second, make sure that both of you are prepared when you get together. It is most effective to learn the fundamentals on your own and use the joint study time to refine your knowledge and help each other with the fine points. If both people are not equally prepared, you either just become a tutor again or you have to be rude and excuse yourself to go study alone.

Third, do not study with someone for the first time the night before a huge test. Do it two or three nights before. That way, if it doesn't work out, you'll have time to rally and still do well on the exam.

Now that I've made studying with someone sound like a horror show, I will tell you that I had some great success with it. Again, it can be very helpful with the right person. By the way, this person needs to be someone you're comfortable enough with to tell her if the session is not helping you. When it happens, you need to be able to tell her that you want to study with her next time around, but that you need to go solo on that particular night. Remember, the goal is for it to work for <u>you</u>.

In closing, let me mention that hiring a tutor does not count as "studying with someone else." If you've used up your free opportunities, office hours and test preparation sessions offered by the professor, this can be incredibly helpful. Generally tutors are knowledgeable and can assist you. But like in anything else, there are good tutors and bad tutors. The week before a test is a great time to try a new tutor. The <u>night</u> before is not.

*Study* **SMART** *to succeed.*

# Chapter 19

*Power studying*

# WHEN TO DO IT

*I*t's not enough to know how to study; you need to know when to study. It may not be the difference between passing and failing, but it very well may be the difference between a C and an A or a B in a class. I offer several suggestions here.

Let's start with when NOT to study. The answer — all night. Pulling an "all nighter," literally staying up all night to study for a test, is nothing short of crazy. At midnight, you drink eight Mountain Dews and eat three bags of Doritos to help you stay awake. As a result, you get a sort of glazed, wild-eyed look by about 2:00 a.m. By 4:00 a.m., the caffeine from the last 6 cans has kicked in and you're reading 14 pages a minute. By 6:00 a.m. the caffeine is wearing off and you find your face falling into your notebook. By 8:00 a.m., you hit a brick wall. Your head is swimming. You're a little sick to your stomach (what a surprise after how well you've treated your body), and you're so exhausted you hardly know what five plus five equals. It's now time to go take your test. Gee, I wonder how you'll do.

Have you ever seen an athlete go through sleep deprivation the night before the big game? Does a politician stay up all night before his big debate? Does a company's CEO go sleepless before her annual meeting with the Board of Directors? Of course not. It would be ludicrous. How is an all nighter before a test any different? Simply put, it's not. It's suicide. It's stupid. Don't do it.

***The classic all nighter.***

Get at least four hours of sleep the night before the test and you'll perform better. If you run out of time, you may not get to review those final two chapters of the book. But, at least you'll remember your "notes-notes," your notes, and the six or seven chapters you did review.

After staying up all night, you'll likely remember less of everything and your ability to reason your way to answers you're unsure of will be severely diminished. Remember, college tests are designed to make you think.

Also, remember to watch your caffeine. It can be very effective in helping to keep you mentally focused if you are wearing down. But

 just because some is good <u>does</u> <u>not</u> mean more is better. Too much caffeine will make you jittery and actually hurt your ability to concentrate. Several hours later when you come back down off the ceiling you'll realize that you've accomplished very little. Moderation is the key.

By the way, I do think people lie about their study habits. They think it's very hip to be able to say that they pulled an all nighter. It's not "hip." It's stupid.

To avoid putting yourself in a position where your back is up against the wall, I'd recommend doing your "notes-notes" three or four days before an exam. You may not need to study three or four days for it, but this first step will give you a good feel for how much material you need to know, how complex it is, and how well you currently know it.

If you have a question, you'll also be much more likely to be able to get to your professor either in class or during office hours to have it answered. If you wait until the day before to begin your effort, you have literally no chance of getting her help.

In general, though, plan on studying a lot more than you did in high school. There will be much, much more information to soak up as, generally speaking, you'll move more quickly through material and take exams less often when you are in college. You'll also spend very little time in the class reviewing for the test. You're pretty much on your own.

There is no good specific answer to the question of how much studying is enough. Every class is different and so is every student. Just start early and keep working at it until you feel like you have a good grasp of the subject matter. You'll know when you're ready.

What part of the day to study is another consideration. As I mentioned earlier, I'm a big believer in studying between classes at the library. Unfortunately, that won't be enough for a big test. Know yourself. Some people are morning people. Some people are night people. Study during the part of the day when you are most alert and most productive. It sounds simple enough, but a lot of people don't do it. It's much trendier to be able to say you stayed up until 4:00 a.m. studying than to say that you got up at 6:00 a.m. to hit the books.

How many beers to have before studying is another decision point. You know the answer so I won't have to sound like your mom or dad again by telling you. When you're working, work. When you're having fun, have fun. Mixing the two is not really that fun and it's not at all effective.

**STUDYING** *at optimal times* **WILL MAKE A DIFFERENCE. TAKE ADVANTAGE OF IT** *and help separate yourself from the pack.*

# WHERE TO DO IT

*A*lso under the subject of "sounds simple enough," you need to study in the right environment. Study in a quiet place where there will be no interruptions. You could study eight hours in front of the TV or two hours in the corner of the top floor of the library, and you'll most likely do better in the latter case. And realistically speaking, you weren't having that much fun in front of the TV with your Sociology notes in your lap.

***Studying at its lowest level.***

An uncrowded corner of the library is a good choice, or any truly remote place you can find. Key here is to make your study time as productive as you can. That way you'll need less of it. Three horrible places to study are 1) with chatty friends, 2) in a fraternity or sorority house, and 3) in a part of the library with lots of walk-by traffic. All of these would be more enjoyable than highly effective studying, but you'll get nothing done from a studying standpoint and won't have as much fun as you would have if you were fully focused on having fun during that period of time. Poor time management.

Let me elaborate on the area of the library with lots of walk-by traffic – the "social section." If you go to the library and park yourself in the social section, you are significantly hurting your odds of success on the upcoming exam. Hey, I think the social section is great. You won't find a better place for conversation or to meet a date for next Saturday night. There is an opportunity in every other seat. Just don't study there!

If you really, really want to be in the social section, you can use a 15 minute trip there as a reward for two hours straight of intensive effort in the corner of the library basement. It can be a bit of incentive to help you produce good, lengthy stretches of quality study time. The short visit will also make you feel good about the study progress you are making relative to your classmates.

One other bad place to study is within 100 miles of other people who are taking the same class and are less prepared than you are. Run from them. Hide from them. Do anything you can to stop them from getting to you. They'll want to ask you lots of questions, borrow your notes to copy them, or just talk for 15 minutes about how tough the class is and how unprepared they are. Avoid this whole ordeal. Find a quiet, out-of-the-way place.

One quiet study location that can be good or bad depending on the individual is in bed. If the room is quiet, some people can intensely focus in this comfortable setting. Under the same conditions, others will fall asleep in 10 minutes or less. If you're going to try this one, don't do it when you're tired or the night before a big test. Try it several nights before and see how it works.

If you follow this advice, you'll not only improve your academic performance, you'll have more free time to pursue other more enjoyable endeavors, however you may define that. If you want to, during your free time you can grab a miscellaneous textbook, go to the social section of the library, and spend as much time there as you'd like.

*You won't be hurting any other student's* **CHANCE OF SUCCESS** *by being in the social section. They're not getting anything done anyway!*

# Chapter 21

# TESTS

*B*efore I get into this chapter, I'll let you know that I'm making the assumption that you've studied adequately. If you haven't studied, you're dead. It's that simple. The techniques I'll share with you will give you an extra edge, not resurrect you from the dead.

The methods I'll share do work well. But, if you had straight A's in high school, don't completely abandon your old test taking techniques. They seem to be working okay for you so far!

*If you don't study, you're dead.*

Okay, here we go. When you first get the exam, take two minutes and scan the whole test. Ask yourself if you'll be pressured for time or if you'll have time to thoroughly think through and answer each question. Will it be a bear or a breeze? Obviously, the tests that are both lengthy and difficult are the most troublesome. Regardless, you'll know what you're up against immediately.

After looking over the test, if it looks long or tough, don't panic. Sitting there staring at it in shock for 15 minutes will do you no good!

Start easy – go to the questions you're sure you can answer correctly. This will do two things. First, you'll pick up the sure points. If you run out of time, you'll have skipped the difficult questions rather than the "gimmes." Second, you'll generate some positive momentum for yourself.

Once you know you've picked up 35 or 40 of a possible 100 points in the first 10 minutes, you'll be calm and confident. You'll be panicky and rushed if you spend the time struggling through questions you're unsure of.

Next, move to remaining high value questions, the ones worth the most points. You'll want to have time to <u>think</u> through these. How long it takes to answer a question is not always related to how much it's worth.

If the values are not spelled out, the simplest, best approach is to hit the easy questions first, then go from top to bottom. Just don't spend too much time thinking about a question you are clueless about. You can do this at the end of the test if time permits.

If the test is multiple choice, proper procedure can make a tremendous difference in your results. After you read each question, try to answer it mentally before you read the given answer options. This will allow you to potentially crystallize your thoughts before being confused by potential trick answers. Then read all the answers to ensure that you've made the right choice. If you draw a blank, think of the question as multiple elimination. Read the answers, immediately eliminating the choices that you know aren't correct.

On most tests, there are usually only two reasonable answers to a question. By using the elimination process, you've got a 50% chance of getting the question right even if you haven't got a clue.

On an essay test, the rules change completely. The objective here is to download every possible thing in your brain on the subject area onto the piece of paper. No points are awarded for impressive sentence structure (unless it's an English class). And, you get no extra points for being brief and "to the point" on an essay test.

In grading an essay test, a professor is looking for some specific points within your answer. For each one she finds, you get points. Key vocabulary words and catch phrases will be critical to you. Use them wherever and whenever you can work them in. When grading 400 handwritten tests, the professor (or her assistant) can get tired and a bit sloppy. In that case, the vocabulary words and catch phrases can add 10 to 15% to your test score.

Obviously, the essay test favors the individual with a full mind and a fast pen. Think through the answer to a question before putting pen to paper. Then, put your head down and don't stop writing until the bell rings and the class is over. One almost painfully obvious point related to this is that your writing must be legible. The mood of a professor grading these hundreds of tests can go sour in a hurry when she has to spend extra time deciphering your "chicken scratch."

If you don't understand a question on a test, ask the professor to rephrase it for you. You won't be able to do this in every situation, and, some professors won't answer a question during a test. But you've got nothing to lose, and in many cases it will be the difference between getting the answer right and wrong. In fact, another reason to ask is that professors will often inadvertently give you clues to the correct answer in attempting to clarify the question for you.

Another key point on test taking – DON'T CHEAT. I know I sound like I'm preaching again, but I've seen people get caught. It's ugly. Even if cheat sheets were your bread and butter in high school, let me bluntly tell you that the stakes here are significantly higher, so you'll need to change your approach.

If you're caught, in a best case scenario you'll get a 0 for the test or may get kicked out of the class. The F will go onto your transcripts and will seriously damage your grade point. And, you're probably going to have to explain it to someone (like a prospective employer) somewhere down the line. If you're less fortunate you'll be put on probation or

*A really bad idea.*

kicked out of school.

Said another way, colleges take it fairly seriously. If you get caught, you're fried. It's just not worth it.

One final thought. You can pick up some additional points after the test if you have developed a strong relationship with your professor. Go see her and talk to her about any points of disagreement you have on how she graded your test. If you thought a multiple choice question had two correct answers, make the point.

If you think she misunderstood your essay answer, it is certainly worth a discussion. Be prepared, do it professionally and with a cool head, and sometimes you can pick up some critical points – if you have laid the groundwork beforehand and have a good relationship with her.

*And remember, a* **COOL HEAD** *and a* **LITTLE SLEEP** *will* *always* **WORK BETTER THAN** *the* **ALTERNATIVES.**

# *Finals*

# WEEK(S)

*C*ollege tests can be tough. In classes in your major or those designed to "weed out" people who want to get into a popular major, they're even tougher. Even with the study and test taking skills you've learned thus far, you'll need to plan to study a great deal to do well on <u>one</u> test. In fact, college exams in any class you'll take will be challenging relative to what you've seen in the past.

College finals are even harder. A typical test will most likely be cumulative, covering not just six or eight weeks of material, but the information covered in an entire semester (or quarter). And, just to make it interesting, you'll have to take <u>five</u> finals during the same week, probably all between Monday and Thursday. It's a little thing called "finals week."

In a matter of 100 hours or so, your grade point could go from a 3.0 to a 4.0 <u>or</u> a 2.0. Words like "challenging" do not begin to explain what you'll be up against.

To say that nothing you have previously experienced in your academic life has prepared you for this tremendous personal battle would be accurate... perhaps a bit of an understatement, but accurate nonetheless.

Do I have your attention?

I thought so.

Done right, finals week can be an opportunity to make a semester of intelligent study habits pay off with a strong boost to your G.P.A. Done wrong, well, let's not talk about that.

Let's talk about how to make it work for you.

First, think about the experience as finals week<u>s</u>. It's a two week process that starts the Monday <u>before</u> you take your first test.

Second, determine how much studying you'll need to do. Make an educated guess as to how many hours you'll need to study for each specific test. If you've been to class, have the notes, have the "notes-notes," and have done the reading work that was absolutely necessary, I would guess you'll need 12-15 hours per class. This will vary by individual and by class.

In going through this process, you'll know how many study hours you'll need to spend in total to be prepared to do well on <u>all</u> your tests. And, doing it the Monday before finals week will give you the opportunity to make the necessary time commitment to put in the required hours to get the job done right.

Finally, make a day-to-day schedule and stick to it. Include things on the schedule like going to class, eating, sleeping, doing laundry, etc. You <u>will</u> need to do these things. Add any study sessions your professors are offering. Then, fill in the schedule with your proposed study time by subject area (i.e., Tuesday 1:00-4:00 Calculus).

One thing that may help you will be the scheduling of your tests during finals week. If you have no tests on Thursday and only one on Friday, you can possibly do all your studying for that test after you are done with the others on Wednesday.

Make your study schedule starting with your last test first and work your way back in reverse order from there. This will leave you with the most sensible possible study schedule for the two week period.

You should also plan to study for a given final the last couple of hours before you go take it. It will get you focused, build your confidence, and keep the material top of mind in your short term memory. Believe me, you'll need it.

You may find when you put together this schedule that you'll have virtually no time to do much else in the next 10 days. If that's the case, you know what your priority needs to be. You may also find that you have some time each day in the first week for a good study break... be it a movie, a game of basketball, or a trip to the bagel shop. That's great.

You will clearly, however, know what you'll need to do to get the job done. You'll also know that you'll have some time off <u>after</u> finals to catch your breath. You'll need it!

A couple of other points.

Don't make the experience a two week sleep deprivation experiment. Your body can't perform well under that scenario. Make sure you're getting at least six hours of sleep a night in week one and at least four hours a night during the actual finals week. This may vary. Know your own body and make intelligent decisions.

You'll also have a bit more study time during finals week than during a typical week. Why? Because you don't have to go to class. It will provide you with some extra quality hours that you'll probably desperately need at that point in time.

Of course, the other key to success is to stay calm. If your study schedule is realistic and you follow it, you'll be fine. Freaking out will not in any way assist you in the process.

Just keep a cool head and put in the necessary time.

*You'll be* **SURPRISED**

*at how well you'll do.*

## Section

# VI

# *The Winning Edge Extracurriculars*

*Y*ou got the grades.

You got the big interview.

It's show time and you're so close to getting your dream job that you can taste it. You go into the interview and begin to get BOMBARDED with questions. The interviewer wants concrete examples of when you exhibited **Leadership** to make an organization truly better, of when you showed **Entrepreneurship** to change the status quo, of how you used **Logic** to get out of a tough jam, and of when you showed **Communication** and **Group skills** in working with others.

Are you rock solid or collapsing under the barrage?

If you haven't been heavily involved in extracurricular activities, you're going to crumble. You have no answers, and you have no job.

There's no <u>one</u> magic club, honorary, or other extracurricular activity that every employer is looking for. Virtually any organization can provide you with an

*Virtually any organization can provide you with an opportunity to build your resumé*

opportunity to build your resumé. So make the **Effort** and get involved in something you think you'll enjoy and be good at. It can be anything from student government to a meaningful club membership. And, if you get involved in numerous groups and keep your grades up, you will strongly demonstrate your **Organizational skills**. It's up to you how to do it. Just get involved!

And remember, if you don't have a strong extracurricular record, your interviews will most likely be filled with silence or shallow conversation. Unless you're strong here or have incredible work experience (we'll talk about that later), you'll have <u>nothing</u> to talk about. And, you won't be able to prove that you have the Winning Characteristics.

## Someone else will get
# YOUR DREAM JOB.

# *Chapter 2:*

# YOUR MARK

*M* aking significant differences in organizations or in a workplace setting during college is not a nice extra — it's a <u>must</u>. I CANNOT emphasize that point enough.

Focusing for now on non-work experiences, you can make your mark through organizations related to your field of study, student government, the fraternity/sorority system, charitable groups, community involvement, or in a variety of other ways. I know of no other way to better prove that you have the Winning Characteristics than by pursuing extracurriculars.

Let me clarify what I mean by "making your mark" or "making significant differences." Boiling it down, a group needs to be <u>meaningfully</u> better because you were a part of it. Another way to think about it would be to ask yourself the question, "What good things would <u>not</u> have happened if you were not a part of the group?"

Okay, so how do you make your mark?

It doesn't happen overnight. You have to first join an

organization and commit enough time to understand it in detail. As you grasp the fundamentals, think about how you can make it better. Looking at it from another angle, try to figure out what is stopping the organization from being as good as it can possibly be. Ask current and past leaders of the group what they think the key opportunities are. Talk to any other relevant people on campus to get their perspective.

After doing some research and giving it some thought, you should be able to develop a plan as to how you're going to make your mark.

From there, you'll need to convince the group that your idea is the right thing to do, get them to rally behind you, and make it a reality. You may have to start small to prove that your ideas are good and that you're committed enough to pull them off. Once you build credibility, the sky is the limit! You could even end up running the group. From there, you can really make things happen.

If at all possible, it's very helpful if you can somehow prove the organization was tangibly better from your efforts (i.e., more members, better financial position, better programs). This type of ammunition is your ticket to the dream job in an interview situation.

See, making your mark is simple. Okay, it's not simple, but it is incredibly important.

As you think about how you might do this, it's important that you know that you do not have to accomplish show-stopping, dramatic, Guiness-Book-of-World-Record type things in making your mark. You just need to make some positive differences. Let me give you a few examples from my college experience.

I joined the Kappa Sigma fraternity at Miami. I never planned to get involved in the Greek system, but since it was the center of the school's social activity, it made sense. After I joined, I saw an opportunity to help improve the small, struggling organization and got heavily involved to do so.

I became social chairman during my sophomore year and threw some great parties that were well attended and that helped build our reputation on campus. During junior year, I was elected President and set out to significantly improve the fraternity for the long term. Working with the other elected officers, I came up with some new ideas and generated support for them with our members. **(Leadership)**

For instance, we tightened up our standards and changed the criteria for who we were going to let join the fraternity. No longer would someone get in simply because he was a nice guy, we had room for him in the house, and needed the money he would pay for room and board. From then on, the applicants had to be strong scholastically, socially, athletically, or in some other way to join the organization.

We wanted individuals representing the fraternity to be leaders on campus if the group was going to be as strong as it could be. Thinking **Logically**, we decided that if we wanted to attract quality, we had to be quality.

This was a tough financial decision. We had to tighten our belt the first year when we limited admission to eight pledges (versus a typical class of 20). It paid off in the second year in the type and number of people who joined, and the fraternity has been more successful ever since. In fact, 10 years later it is now one of the strongest on campus.

You can make your mark in a wide variety of ways. An unorthodox but meaningful example of how I made my mark was my effort related to a "tug-of-war" event on campus. It was an annual competition among all of the 24 fraternities. Okay, it was a bit silly, but half of the campus, about 5,000 people, would come out to watch us grunt a lot, get muddy, tear up our hands, and try desperately to win this contest.

I decided that if we wanted to be seen as a major fraternity on campus, we could give ourselves a shot in the arm if we could do well in this high profile event. Showing **Leadership**, I organized our team and developed a new pulling technique that allowed our small but athletic team to compete against some of the horses we would be up against.

From there, we practiced every night after dinner for two weeks. This was no small task as we had to get 15 guys from the fraternity to pull against the 10 of us who would represent our organization in the event.

We beat one of the biggest houses on campus and came in fifth place out of 24 teams. Not bad for a small fraternity. In our second year, we beat the defending champs and came in second place, receiving a standing ovation from the huge crowd (and achieving our goal of improving our image on campus).

*You can make an impact in any number of ways.*

Okay, this wasn't rocket science. In fact, it was a tremendous amount of fun. But it did show interviewers that I was **Entrepreneurial** enough to come up with a way to use an existing event as a way to build our image, had enough **Logic** to come up with an innovative pulling technique, had the **Group skills** to get 25 guys to actively participate, and was willing to put forth the **Effort** to pull it off. And, we were successful in achieving our goal.

It's exactly the kind of stuff interviewers are looking for!

An example more directly related to my future career was a marketing program I put together for a local restaurant during my senior year. I did it as a part of my involvement in a marketing group, Pi Sigma Epsilon. I joined the group because I knew I could use more experience in the marketing area.

A restaurant owner called us for some free advice on how he could improve his business. It was not a high priority project for the group, so I had the opportunity to **lead** it, even as a newcomer. After doing some research, we developed a comprehensive proposal on how we thought he could improve his business. The owner successfully used some of the ideas. The business became more profitable, and I had another positive Winning Characteristics story to share during interviews.

Another area loaded with opportunities to make your mark is community service. This type of involvement is extremely impressive on a resumé and is a legitimate way for you to go out and do a little bit of good in the world. An **Entrepreneurial** example here could be the setting up of a successful student Red Cross blood drive or United Way campaign that had not been previously undertaken – or the significant improvement of one already in place. You'd be amazed at the reaction that a successful program of this type would generate.

Today's professionals in all fields want their organizations to be seen as good civic contributors. If they think you can help with this, it could give you an important edge.

Focus on quality, not quantity in this resumé building process. Making a significant contribution to two or three groups is much more meaningful than being a weak, non-contributing member of 17 different groups. REMEMBER, UNLESS YOU DO SOMETHING IN ORGANIZATIONS YOU JOIN, YOU STILL HAVE NOTHING TO TALK ABOUT ON INTERVIEW DAY.

As you think about what you'll pursue, don't focus on only one group. If you don't get elected to a key position or things don't work out for one reason or another, you'll want to have some other options available.

And, the organizations don't have to be the most popular ones on campus. Interviewers care much more about what you did to improve, build, or change the group for the better than they do about which organizations they were. Again, they're just looking for evidence of the Winning Characteristics.

A key point in being able to make your mark is to start early. If you want to prove yourself, get elected to a key office, and perform at a high level to make a real difference, you'll need to be in that group for two or three years. That means you should start, at the latest, at the beginning of your sophomore year.

It may even be worth considering starting your own organization if you see an opportunity to do so. Creating something from nothing is a great challenge and will impressively display all of the Winning Characteristics.

Non-group activities can also be a plus. I tutored economics during my junior and senior years. I didn't spend a tremendous amount of time doing it. But, it suggested that I was at least relatively intelligent (**Logic**), and could **Communicate** with others. As a part of an overall record of achievement, small things will make a difference.

And remember, it's important to get involved in something that you are sincerely interested in. You're going to put in some major time and **Effort,** and you'll work harder and perform better if you care about what you're doing. If you aren't committed, it will be obvious to your fellow members, and you won't have much hope of being a leader or making much of a difference.

# SO GET INVOLVED.

*Or get left behind in your future job hunt.*

# Chapter 24

# *Clubs and*

# HONORARIES

*C*lubs and honoraries are a real mixed bag. They can be extremely helpful or a complete waste of time and money. The right ones can open doors for you. The wrong ones are no more than a way to spend $75, get a pin that you'll never wear again, and put some Greek letters on your resumé.

The definition of an honorary versus a club can vary greatly by organization. Typically, an honorary is a group that offers you an invitation to join based on some type of achievement (e.g., good grades or service). A club will grant membership for an endless number of reasons depending on the type of group it is and how exclusive it's attempting to be.

A specific club or honorary can be a great opportunity or a complete waste of time. You'll need to "scratch below the surface" before joining to see if a specific group is worth your time (and money).

Good ones are an outstanding opportunity for you to exhibit the Winning Characteristics if you take a leadership position in them and make something good happen out of it.

As I mentioned, I was a member of a marketing club called Pi Sigma Epsilon my junior and senior years. Big deal, right? While some interviewers hadn't heard of it, it gave me an accomplishment to talk about in my interviews. It's a terrific example of the fact that an action oriented group will take you a lot farther than one that has a fancy name and gives you a pin to put in your drawer. It also demonstrates that it's more important <u>what you do</u> in an organization versus which one you do it in.

Clubs and honoraries related to your major are generally a good opportunity. If you haven't already done so, stop by the department office for your major to find out what's available and what the criteria are to join each group.

These organizations will help educate you on the range of jobs available in your field. They'll also introduce you to potential employers and give you the opportunity to begin to build important relationships well before your first interview. If you can use them as a way to demonstrate the Winning Characteristics, all the better.

The accounting honorary I was a member of, Beta Alpha Psi, held monthly receptions hosted by large accounting firms that interviewed at our school. It gave me a great opportunity to meet some key people and find out what each company had to offer in terms of types of jobs, salaries, working environment, and potential for advancement. Key to mention, though, is that the most helpful honoraries are not typically open to all students. You need good grades to get into them.

Fraternities and sororities are a whole different kind of "club." As I mentioned, I never thought I would join a fraternity. But I ended up doing so on a whim, and it turned out to be one of the best decisions I made in college. Fraternities and sororities are loaded with opportunities for you to build and exhibit the Winning Characteristics. They tend to have five or so elected officers and another 10 to 15 positions of responsibility in the organization. Each of them is an opportunity to shine.

But beware. Almost every fraternity and sorority has a group of hardcore "partyers" who slide through with a C average and have a great time. They are a lot of fun but don't seem to have nearly as good a time living back at home washing dishes for a living after college.

*You get what you earn.*

There are many ways to get involved and make a real contribution with any legitimate club or honorary. With elected and appointed positions, you can always find a way to make an impact at some level. If you do a good job, the opportunities will grow from there. It will be whatever you make of it.

On a less positive note, I have found no value whatsoever in paying $75 to be in something like the Sophomore Scholastic Honorary. You go to a ceremony, pay your money, get your pin and certificate, and get the right to put some Greek letters on your resumé. A recruiter will care less. Or worse yet, they'll ask you about your involvement in and contribution to the group. Good luck answering that one!

I feel the same way about the "Who's Who" books. You get your name in a big book with many other people and get the opportunity to buy it for $50. Awfully impressive, isn't it?

Clubs and honoraries can be of real benefit. Let me restate that. They can be of real benefit <u>if</u> you take the time and effort to make a true impact – to once again exhibit that you have the Winning Characteristics.

**JUST STAY AWAY** *from*

*the cheesy, transparent,*

**RESUMÉ FILLER STUFF.**

# Chapter 2

# On Organized

# SPORTS

**D**oes anybody really care if you're the second string center fielder on your college baseball team?

Well, actually, they do.

Sure, you'd be better off if you were the starting quarterback on its winningest football team in history, but not everybody can do that. Regardless, there are some real positives to being involved in athletics at the intercollegiate or "club" level (or even the intramural level).

First of all, most people inherently like athletes. Maybe it's not fair, but it's a reality. We're a sports-crazed culture, so being a jock can give you a leg up.

Athletic participation also shows you are willing to put forth tremendous **Effort** to succeed. To do well, you have to be self disciplined enough to keep working at it. You can't be a quitter. Interviewers like that.

Most sports allow you to exhibit your **Group skills** by being a contributing team player. This includes things like making personal sacrifices for the good of the group. It involves cooperating with fellow team members that aren't necessarily your best friends.

And, it's another way to develop and demonstrate **Communication skills**. It's tough to be effective on a team without them.

Contrary to popular belief, participation in competitive intercollegiate sports gives you a chance to show that you possess **Logic**. Most sports at the college level involve strategy and require you to be able to think well under pressure to succeed. You need a little more than to be able to throw a football well to excel in NCAA sports.

It also takes some strong **Organizational skills**. College sports take up a great deal of time, forcing you to be relatively organized to survive your classes, much less maintain a good grade point average.

For intercollegiate sports, in season, you can plan on a commitment of two to five hours per day. Big school or small, they take their athletics seriously. And, most sports have "home" and "away" events. When you have "away" games or matches, it will be an even bigger time commitment, sometimes taking up a full day or even an entire weekend. And don't count on a whole lot of sympathy from your professors. Even if you're the next Michael Jordan, you won't get it at most schools.

You'll need to be priority focused and a good time manager to keep your grades up during these peak periods. You may even consider scheduling your most difficult classes around your athletics. Take them, if possible, during the off season.

If you are a very good athlete but not able to compete at the intercollegiate level, "club" sports may be an option to consider. Club sports are generally well organized with many of the characteristics of intercollegiate athletics. You'll practice, have an official schedule, and compete against different schools. The quality of the competition will still be quite good and the time commitment will still be rather heavy. But, it can be a great deal of fun and will allow you to exhibit the same characteristics as varsity level NCAA sports.

Finally, on a level that most of us can relate to, even participation on your dormitory corridor's intramural softball team will help you in your pursuit. Along with allowing you to show you are a good team player (among other things), it will allow you the chance to relax, take a break from your busy schedule, and get in a workout.

And, who knows, the company you're interviewing with may need a good shortstop for its co-rec softball team!

*So, don't overlook organized sports if* **YOU'RE SWINGING FOR THE FENCE.**

**Personal**

*Chapter 26*

# FITNESS

*P*articipation in intramural sports or any other sports related activity offers yet one more important benefit – it keeps you physically fit.

As I once again step into the land of the politically incorrect, let me state that recruiters like candidates who look like they make an attempt to take care of themselves. If you ever asked them about it, they would most certainly deny it. Regardless, it is a fact of life.

They're not looking for body builders or beauty queens. They don't care if you're tall or short, or have a large or small frame. Fifteen percent body fat or less is not a requirement to be hired by any firm. But, you can help your cause by giving the impression that you make an effort to take care of your body.

Is this fair? No. Does it happen? Yes. Could you ever prove it? Probably not. The interviewer probably doesn't even know that he or she is doing it.

Are physically fit people more energetic and motivated than people who are not? Do they have more discipline and self control and therefore make better employees? Who knows! Every person is different. But, if you will be perceived better if you are in shape, isn't it worth the effort?

Someone who exercises regularly is also a better risk from a health standpoint. This is of major interest to some employers. In fact, many companies build fitness centers for their employees to encourage them to work out (cutting future medical costs). Other organizations will reimburse staff for membership in a local fitness club. Fitness is no longer a "craze." It's here to stay.

Get in shape. It's a "healthy" way to impress an employer.

*Just* **GET AND STAY IN SHAPE**

*and you may have a leg up on*

*interview day.*

# *Chapter 27*

# YOUR WORLD

*T*here's a whole world out there... and you ought to know at least a little bit about it.

You don't need to become obsessed with it, but you should dedicate at least a couple of hours each week to understanding current events in the news. Make the effort to expand your world with some outside reading or news oriented TV. It will probably be a little painful at first, but it's well worth your time.

I say this for a couple of reasons. First, you'll learn from it and, in general, be a more well rounded person. It sounds a bit corny, but you'll gain a lot of knowledge that can benefit you in a multitude of ways. Second, (and more consistent with the book), it may be important in helping you achieve your career objectives.

If you're at a pre-interview reception or out to dinner with a potential employer, it is crucial. You'll come off as smart, mature, and well rounded, and you'll have something to talk about other than the outstanding party you attended last weekend.

Seriously, if you're standing there for 15 minutes talking to a 52 year old corporate recruiter who did not attend your school and is from a different part of the country, you <u>need</u> something to talk about!

In fact, many recruiters will look almost as heavily at their discussion with you in this informal setting as they will at an interview. In their mind, it's a way to see you in a "real life" setting.

Publications like *Time, Newsweek, U.S. News and World Report, Wall Street Journal,* and *USA Today* offer excellent introductory rates for college students. Take advantage of the opportunity. Go in halves with your roommate or a friend down the hall. It's worth the money.

If you just can't swing it financially, go to the library and read there, plan to regularly tune into CNN Headline News, or get on the internet to get some perspective on what's going on "off campus."

One final point. If you subscribe to a professional publication related

*A good investment.*

to your major (like the Journal of the American Medical Association) you'll find it to be difficult reading at first.

Stick with it, though. It will get easier. You'll find regular features in a particular publication which seem to relate well to what you're studying. The vocabulary you pick up will be helpful, too.

**EXPANDING YOUR WORLD** *is a* **GOOD INVESTMENT** – *of your time and your money.*

# Section

# *Working toward success*

*I*f you're still pressing ahead toward completing this book, you'll probably have "a great job after college" as a personal goal.

Work experience along the way can be a major plus toward ultimately getting to do the work you want after graduation. With the <u>right</u> work, it is an outstanding opportunity to prove that you possess all of the Winning Characteristics.

I'll categorize work in three separate groups – jobs during college, summer jobs, and internships.

CAREER

COMMUNICATION · ORGANIZATION · LEADERSHIP · LOGIC · EFFORT · GROUP SKILLS · ENTREPRENEUR

WORK EXPERIENCE

Each type of work has value. Some offer significantly more than others. Certain jobs, while having value, are actually more of a detriment than a benefit if you look at how they will help you toward your "great job after college" goal.

*Work experience along the way can be a major plus.*

## So if and when you work,
# WORK TOWARD SUCCESS.

# COLLEGE

*Jobs during*

*W*hen I talk about working during school, I'm not referring to summer vacation or Christmas break but while classes are in session. For most college students, working during summer break to help cover expenses is somewhat of a given. By the way, I think working your tail off at lousy jobs during the summer provides good perspective on life. I'll get into that in the next chapter.

Working while school is in session is a somewhat "dicey" subject as people work during this time frame for two fundamentally different reasons. The first is to be able to survive – to pay tuition and eat (two fairly noble causes). The second reason students work is for extra spending money for pizza and to go out on the weekend (these too can be argued to be at least somewhat noble causes).

If you're working because you don't have a choice financially, the decision is rather simple – do it. I say this for two reasons. First, you have no other option. It is how you are going to get through college and it will certainly be a character builder. Second, there is something quite compelling to an interviewer about students who wanted so badly to get an education that they got incredibly **Organized** and put forth the **Effort** necessary to successfully take on the challenge of working full-time while carrying heavy college course loads. It's the "American Dream" happening in a fundamental way. It's impressive.

If you do need to work, make every attempt to do it in a job that is a step in the direction of your future career. It will give you a look at what you might actually be doing after you graduate and will help convince your potential future employer (and yourself) that you have some talent in, and liking for, this field in a non-academic, "real world" setting. If you want to be a pediatric nurse, it will be more helpful to work at a day care center than to paint houses for a builder.

If you don't truly need to work to pay for school, I would recommend doing so only if it results in <u>significant</u> resumé building. Flipping burgers to be able to afford a better brand of beer and a few extra pizzas is a <u>really</u>, <u>really</u>, <u>really</u> bad idea. (Am I making my point?) The time you spend doing this is completely wasted and will do you no good at interview time. In fact, it will come to be a significant disadvantage to you as you'll be competing against students who were doing something beneficial with their time.

Temporary "poverty" in college is a lot better than overcommitment to a frivolous endeavor that will get you no points on interview day. Besides, you can go out every night and overdose on pizza <u>after</u> you land your dream job.

One way you can work that <u>can</u> be a very effective use of your time (and be a lot of fun) is starting your own business. Whether it be a company designing and selling novelty T-shirts and boxer shorts, painting houses, or making and selling flower arrangements, starting your own business is a great way to exhibit the Winning Characteristics.

Let me explain how starting your own business can help you show you possess these characteristics. While he was a sophomore at Harvard, my friend Brad Baker identified an opportunity in the Boston market and decided to start a T-shirt company to make a few extra bucks.

Among other things, he had to develop the designs, research the production process, contract with a manufacturer, figure out who would buy these shirts, determine what price he could sell them for, where he could legally sell them, who would sell them for him and at what wage. He also needed to figure out how to pay for his upfront printing costs. He undoubtedly ran across a number of other barriers and needed to find a way to effectively work through them.

The fact that he did all this to establish the business, made intelligent decisions along the way, and brought the shirts to market — that's a big time accomplishment! He had undoubtedly in some way demonstrated that he had each of the seven Winning Characteristics. The fact that he actually made a few bucks was all the better.

*So if you're going to work during school, have a good reason for doing so.*

# WORK TOWARD SUCCESS.

# *Chapter 29*

# JOBS

$S$ummer jobs are a way of life for most college students. The money earned in three months of intense work effort helps to support them for the other nine.

The money earned is definitely an important benefit of these efforts. The job may also offer you a type of incentive you may not have considered. The memory of working 12 hour midnight shifts in a 95 degree building stacking paper on the end of a loud, dirty printing press for $5.50 an hour is a great incentive to study hard when you're back at school.

Trust me, I've done it. And, if you don't make good decisions while at college, you may be getting an early preview of your future job. Not necessarily a pretty thought.

You'll have opportunities to develop and provide concrete examples of the Winning Characteristics even with the most unlikely job. In three months of work, you'll certainly have some new ideas and thoughts that are a step forward for the organization.

If you work the same summer job for several years,

***Summer job or a preview of your career?***

you'll have an even greater opportunity to make an impact. If nothing else, you can certainly exhibit that you're a disciplined, hard worker who will put forth great **Effort** to succeed. And, you'll get a strong reference for your future resumé from your boss if you do good work.

By the way, every employer is looking for cost savings opportunities. Many even financially reward employees who can come up with them. Challenge yourself to develop a less expensive way to do what you're doing and present it to your management. Even if they don't pursue it, the fact that you exhibited that type of **Entrepreneurship** can be good ammunition on interview day.

If you can get a job related to your planned career field, it is definitely an added bonus. You'll learn a great deal about what the field is like in the "real world" as opposed to in the classroom. The two can be very, very different. The ultimate chance to do this is an internship.

## INTERNSHIPS *are an* UNBEATABLE *opportunity.*

# Chapter 30

# INTERNSHIPS

*I'*ll be direct here – GET ONE. Internships are an outstanding opportunity and you should do anything possible (within the law) to get one.

They offer you a priceless "test drive" of your chosen field, and you may even get paid to do it. It's a chance to see what it would be like on a day-to-day basis prior to doing it as a graduate. Within this, they also give you meaningful "real world" experience that you will carry back to the classroom and into your next job. They may also take some of the fear out of the thought of entering the "real world" that many students experience.

When you interview for the job you want after graduation, they're quite helpful too. The fact that you pursued an internship shows you'll put forth **Effort** to succeed. And, it will give you meaty, meaningful discussion topics for the interview itself.

The experience could also be an entré into the company with which you interned. Many companies now have internship programs to get a close look at students they think they might like to hire long term. After seeing three or four months of your performance, they can make an informed hiring decision about you for a permanent job.

Even if the internship is not the first step to a full time job opportunity, a letter of recommendation from your internship boss can be a strong vote of confidence in the eyes of any interviewer. If you do utilize a letter of recommendation, you need to be ready to answer the question of why you are not going to work for this highly impressed boss on a full-time basis after graduation. This is not necessarily a problem. You just need to know it's coming.

There are a couple of ways to get an internship. The first is through the school's formal channels, through the Career Planning and Placement Office and via the school's Department Office for your major. Pursue these, but know in advance there will be many applicants going for a limited number of jobs.

Be aggressive about seeking out internships on your own. Send out resumés to local companies. Call the companies and get the names of their personnel directors and department heads. Send out lots of letters and always follow up with a phone call, attempting to set up a meeting to at least talk about what the options may be. Offer to take key contacts to lunch. As busy as they may be, they do eat lunch. You can offer to pay and not be taken up on it in most cases. They have expense accounts and know you don't.

If you meet with potential employers and they're impressed, they may recommend you to another friend in the business if they can't hire you. Don't be shy about asking for other possible employers they may know if they can't offer you anything but seem to like you.

Don't overlook small companies. They may be even more interested than large ones. They may truly <u>need</u> some of your expertise and not be able to afford to hire someone full-time to perform that function. It may not look quite as good as General Motors on your resumé, but you'll probably enjoy a meaningful learning experience that will be as beneficial as one you'd get at a big company. It may also give you a feel for some of the pros and cons of ultimately going to work for a small company versus a big one.

If you don't know what companies are in your town, get a list of Chamber of Commerce members. Try to get an appointment with the Executive Director and let her know how hard you are willing to work and how little you need to be paid. You may ask her to let her Board of Directors know of your interest. A follow up letter from you after the meeting will make this more likely to happen. You will also want to mention that you'd like to work in this area long term. She'll like that.

Use contacts (like your parents, your neighbors, etc.) to get your foot in the door. Look to the parents of your college friends who may work in related fields.

With some **Effort**, you'll find people who will give you a chance. Some of your favorite professors may also be able to help. They have good contacts (past students) and may go to bat for you. Offer to work for a low wage or even free if you can afford to! Some of the best internships available are unpaid positions. And a small company that would love the help but doesn't have the budget for it will be <u>much</u> more likely to give you the opportunity if it doesn't cost any money.

*Just get the experience.*
**IT WILL PAY OFF** *for you*
*in the long run.*

# Section VIII

# *Putting it all together*

*W*ow! It sure sounds complicated. You'll need to do a million different things, including picking the right major, learning how to study in a whole new way, picking professors well, getting into their heads, learning where and how to study, taking tests well, playing organized sports, running an organization, and getting an internship. It's overwhelming!

Actually, it's not all that bad. You <u>can</u> have fun, make some friends for life, <u>and</u> land the job you want. It all comes down to having a good plan.

The next five chapters and Appendix that follow will help simplify what "getting the job done" will mean for you personally. They will also share a semester-by-semester schedule for you to use as a reference guide.

> *It all comes down to having a good plan.*

It's not meant to be followed literally, but instead, to give you some general direction.

Within that, it will give <u>you</u> the opportunity to set some personal goals for yourself. Take the time and

*You can rise above it and succeed.*

make the commitment to complete that exercise.

And finally, you'll get some tips on how long your college experience should last.

## Take them to **HEART.**

# How long it

## Chapter 3

# SHOULD TAKE

*L*et me start by saying that your parents did not pay me to write this chapter. I just happen to have strong feelings on this subject.

Four years.

Not five years.

Not six years.

And certainly not seven.

If it is designed to be a four year program, make a commitment to complete it in four years. It can be done. Really.

If nothing else, think about the cost of the fifth year. First, there's the tuition. Then there's the room and board. Now let's talk about what I'll call the "opportunity loss."

If you would have graduated in four years, you would have been making, not spending money in the fifth year. So, take the actual tuition and room and board costs of the fifth year and add on the $25,000 "opportunity" you gave up by not being out in the "real world" earning it. Your degree will be no more valuable to you than if you get it in four years, it will just cost a lot more for the same piece of paper.

When you think about it that way, the five year plan becomes a little more expensive and a little less attractive, doesn't it?

The other cost associated with the five year plan is what I call the "credibility cost." It is the immediate negative reaction on the part of an interviewer that you were not able to complete your academic program "on time." In a fast paced world with lots of deadlines, this does not give you immediate credibility with the interviewer. You may be able to quickly justify it to them and have a very successful interview. It's just not a great starting point.

As with anything else, there are exceptions to this rule. If you make a significant change in your major during your junior or senior year, take a six to nine month internship, have failing health, financial problems, etc., etc., etc., it may be perfectly legitimate to extend your college experience for another year. And, some programs are <u>designed</u> to be five years in duration and may include a semester abroad to study European architecture and such. These situations can be successfully explained and should not pose a major problem. In fact, a few of the items mentioned will be seen as tremendous assets.

*But, if it's a standard four year program, plan on completing it in four years.*
## IT CAN BE DONE.

# *Chapter 32*

# LOOK AT WHAT
# IT TAKES

*Y*ou're over 140 pages and 30 chapters into the book. Now we'll boil the whole thing down into just a few pages to leave you thinking about how you'll build your future.

If you're going to college to get a great job, you need to understand what an interviewer will be looking for when you get out. They're basically looking for the seven Winning Characteristics:

1. ### COMMUNICATION SKILLS
   being able to make your point in writing and in person.

2. ### ORGANIZATIONAL SKILLS
   being able to get and stay on top of multiple activities.

3. ### LEADERSHIP
   the ability to move a team, to make good things happen.

4. **LOGIC**

good old fashioned smarts and problem solving skills, from analytical ability to creativity.

5. **EFFORT**

a very strong desire to succeed, having the will to win.

6. **GROUP SKILLS**

being a part of the team with an ability to successfully lead <u>and</u> follow.

7. **ENTREPRENEURSHIP**

being a person with new ideas and the ability to make them reality.

To launch your career, you'll need concrete examples of how you have proven that you have these Winning Characteristics. You'll do this in three ways: with strong grades, an impressive record of extracurricular activities, and meaningful work experiences.

From an academic standpoint, a 3.0 average gets you in the game, a 3.5 average puts you in the driver's seat. But don't expect these numbers to come easy.

You'll need to make some very good decisions to achieve them. College isn't easy. It's not supposed to be.

In terms of extracurriculars, it's the quality, not the quantity that will make the difference. Meaningful efforts and contributions will help <u>prove</u> you have the Winning Characteristics.

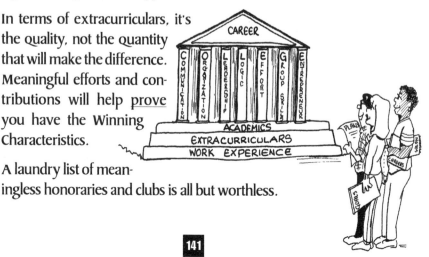

A laundry list of meaningless honoraries and clubs is all but worthless.

Work experience can be a tremendous asset. Internship, in particular, are excellent opportunities to build and exhibit the Winning Characteristics. And, pick summer work and jobs during school wisely to make sure you're "working" toward success.

With good time management, you can accomplish these objectives and still have the time of your life during your college career.

So there it is, your guide to success in college in just a few pages. Think about it, focus on it, and you can make it happen for you.

**IT'S** *not brain surgery. It's* *just* **UNDERSTANDING THE KEYS TO SUCCESS** *and* *making them a part of your* *personal college game plan.*

# Chapter 33

# BY SEMESTER GUIDE

*Y*ou can't wake up the second semester of your senior year and decide you're going to follow the principles in this book. It's too late. The party is over.

An analogy used by the noted author and speaker Dr. Stephen Covey is the "Law of the Harvest." The same principle holds true here. Attempting to accomplish a lot of the principles and objectives spelled out in this book at the very end of your college career would be similar to a farmer planting his corn in August and expecting a good crop in October. He can pull all nighters, fertilizing and watering the crops, giving it 100% to try to catch up. Even though you're probably not a farmer, I bet you're not surprised that this plan won't work too well for him. It's common sense.

Okay then, since success in college is a building process, a bit like growing corn, how can you expect to do well unless you make the effort early and consistently throughout your years there? You can't. I promise you. It just won't work.

Okay, enough with the sermons. Here's the schedule. It's just a guideline, but it will provide you with some important insight. I've done it based on a semester schedule. If you're on quarters, you'll need to make some minor mental adjustments, but the principles still apply.

## Freshman Year - Semester 1

First and foremost, get your feet planted firmly on the ground. This is your opportunity to get adjusted.

Don't be fooled into thinking you can fall behind and catch up later. You can't. About 1 out of 8 students never successfully complete this semester.

Your goal here is <u>not</u> to see how many nights in a row you can party. You will find many people who will tell you it is. Get to know them while you can. They won't be there next semester.

As you settle in, begin to look for a couple of organizations to join, not <u>run</u>, just join.

Find out when fraternity and sorority rush are held. They will be held either once or twice a year. If you're interested in potentially joining, you won't want to miss the dates.

Other organizations you might want to pursue may be related to your major or a hobby interest you have. On-campus bulletin boards and the student newspaper are also excellent ways to learn about extracurricular opportunities.

And, if I haven't mentioned it lately, college is the big leagues. Study hard or you're going to get buried.

## Freshman Year - Semester 2

Okay, you survived. Good for you. Now, where to go from here? If your grades aren't what they need to be, look hard at 1) the level of effort you've <u>truly</u> given, 2) your time management, and 3) the <u>quality</u> of your study technique. Don't give up. You <u>can</u> do it.

Begin to get involved on campus. As I mentioned, just reading the bulletin boards and school paper will make you aware of many opportunities to do so.

And remember, you need to get your grades up to or above 3.0.

## Sophomore Year - Semester 1

You're no longer a rookie. You're now a seasoned veteran. You'll be taking more classes related to your major and digging into some more specialized subject matter.

Begin to attempt to take on responsibility in the organizations you have joined. You're not going to get a top position in these groups until you prove yourself capable in lesser ones.

## Sophomore Year - Semester 2

You ought to be hitting your stride. You now understand how to get the grades and should be making the personal commitment to do so.

If you're not making some progress with extracurriculars, <u>now</u> is the time to start.

If you're thinking about starting up a business or any type of organization, it's not too early to start making plans. By the way, at the end of this semester, you're halfway done!

While most of your major "out of the classroom" achievements are still ahead of you, you ought to have some plans to achieve them pretty well mapped out.

## Junior Year - Semester 1

You're still tracking well academically (if not, <u>memorize</u> chapters 14-22).

You're aggressively working to develop the Winning Characteristics. You'll have some failures along the way, some elections you don't win and some goals you don't achieve. But believe it or not, that is an important part of the learning process.

This is your year for extracurricular accomplishments. Don't let it slip away.

By the way, what are you doing to get an internship?

## Junior Year - Semester 2

If you're not thinking internship, change your thought process. A perfect scenario is a summer job that classifies as one. Get to work, use your contacts, review Chapter 30, and get one!

Keep banging away on projects outside the classroom, and don't let that grade point average slip.

Most of the classes you're taking are in your major. Remember, you want your average in your major to be <u>higher</u> than your overall average.

## Senior Year - Semester 1

In many ways, you're already in your last semester. While you are preparing your resumé and beginning to interview, the real job search flurry will begin next semester.

Said another way, you're in the home stretch. If you don't make some things happen now, they're probably not going to! So get busy or get left behind.

Now it's time to harvest the crop. All of the work you've done will pay off for you in a big way. Be confident. Be aggressive. And go get that job you want.

Interview as much as you can. Work closely with your school's Career Planning and Placement Office to make sure your resumé is well written. It will greatly affect how heavily you are recruited.

Personally contact organizations you would like to work for that are not visiting your school. I've seen that approach pay off many times.

Rather than write another 8 chapters on how to interview, I will simply tell you to utilize all the resources available through your placement office. Be honest, be confident, and sell yourself thoroughly (you've only got one chance to set yourself apart). Make sure the interviewer knows that you <u>really</u> want to work for his or her company.

*You've laid the proper foundation by following the principles in this book so* **YOU SHOULD BE IN EXCELLENT SHAPE.**

# RIGHT NOW

*L*et's talk a bit more about the here and now.

With your 10 year plan in mind from earlier in the book, and with all of the new "wisdom" you now possess, take some time and write down your goals for the next 12 months.

Do it now. Don't wait or you may never do it.

Look at what you will accomplish in terms of academics, involvement in extracurriculars, and other personal or work goals. They don't need to be dramatic. They just have to be realistic, and preferably something you can measure (to know if you achieved them or not). And please, don't forget the "Winning Characteristics."

You can do it right here in the book or in a separate location. Invest a little time in it and then post and track your results.

A couple of hints. Be realistic. Save the thoughts of rock and roll fame for another day. Look at things you have a reasonable shot at accomplishing. They don't all have to be dramatic achievements. Just make sure they are things that are important to you.

Here are a few examples:

Academic

    1.    Miss no more than three classes in a semester.

Extracurricular

    1.    Find and join two organizations related to my major or areas of interest. Go to meetings and volunteer to help.

Work/Personal

    1.    Present at least one new idea a month to my boss on how I can help improve the company.

    2.    Get up by 8:00 a.m. every day Monday through Friday.

Go through the pain. Spend the time. Set some goals related to the Winning Characteristics.

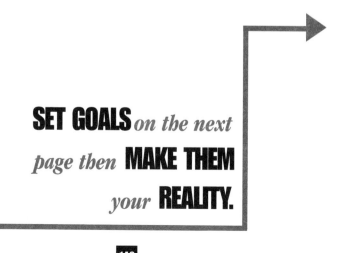

**SET GOALS** *on the next page then* **MAKE THEM** *your* **REALITY.**

# 12 Month Goals/Worksheet

## Academic

1 _____

2 _____

3 _____

4 _____

5 _____

## Extracurricular Activities

1 _____

2 _____

3 _____

4 _____

5 _____

## Work/Personal

1 _____

2 _____

3 _____

4 _____

5 _____

Visit www.makingcollegecount.com
for a free, full-size, printable version of this chart.

# Chapter 35

## Closing

## THOUGHTS

*W*ell, there it is. My definitive guide to making the most of your college experience. Every student is different and every school is different, but on the whole, take the advice and you'll be well ahead in the long run. It works. I'm living proof of it.

I've hit you with a tremendous amount of material. There's no way you could have absorbed all of it. MAKE A PERSONAL COMMITMENT TO READ THE BOOK AGAIN IN SIX MONTHS.

After that period of time, with your additional experiences, you'll read it at a different level and get some additional benefit from it. You may even want to take "notes-notes" next time around and review them every six months to stay on track. It won't take long and certainly can't hurt.

Set goals . Put them somewhere where you'll see them and then make them a reality. It will be rewarding <u>and</u> keep you focused on what's important to <u>you</u>.

Visit our web site. It's a chance to get the latest-and-greatest on the subject of college success (and it will reinforce what you've learned in this book). You can also register for our FREE monthly college success on-line newsletter.

College really is one of the best times in your life. It certainly was for me and should be for you. Just make sure that while you're having all that fun, you're setting yourself up to have the best and most rewarding career possible for the many decades that follow.

# KNOCK 'EM DEAD.

Visit our web site at www.makingcollegecount.com.
It's the world's most comprehensive college success resource.

# APPENDIX

## Your Personal Score sheets

The following sheets will help you track your progress throughout college. They should be a big help in helping you objectively determine if you are "on track" to success. They'll also be a big help when it comes time to put together your resumé and/or application to graduate school.

# Freshman Year

| Class | Professor | Grade |
|-------|-----------|-------|
| | | |
| | | |
| | | |
| | | |
| | | |
| | | |
| | | |
| | | |
| | | |
| | | |
| | | |
| | | |

YEAR END G.P.A. _____

IN MAJOR _____

## Notable Successes

### *Extracurricular*

_____

_____

_____

_____

### *Work Related*

_____

_____

_____

_____

# Sophomore Year

| Class | Professor | Grade |
|-------|-----------|-------|
| | | |
| | | |
| | | |
| | | |
| | | |
| | | |
| | | |
| | | |
| | | |
| | | |
| | | |
| | | |

YEAR END G.P.A. _____

IN MAJOR _____

## Notable Successes

### Extracurricular

_____

_____

_____

_____

### Work Related

_____

_____

_____

_____

# Junior Year

| Class | Professor | Grade |
|-------|-----------|-------|
|       |           |       |
|       |           |       |
|       |           |       |
|       |           |       |
|       |           |       |
|       |           |       |
|       |           |       |
|       |           |       |
|       |           |       |
|       |           |       |
|       |           |       |
|       |           |       |

YEAR END G.P.A. _____

IN MAJOR _____

# Notable Successes

## *Extracurricular*

_____

_____

_____

## *Work Related*

_____

_____

_____

# Senior Year

| Class | Professor | Grade |
|-------|-----------|-------|
| | | |
| | | |
| | | |
| | | |
| | | |
| | | |
| | | |
| | | |
| | | |
| | | |
| | | |

YEAR END G.P.A. _____

IN MAJOR _____

# Notable Successes
## *Extracurricular*

_____

_____

_____

_____

## *Work Related*

_____

_____

_____

_____

# Notes

# Notes

# Notes

# Notes

# Notes